THE **AUDACITY** OF **HOOP**

ALSO BY ALEXANDER WOLFF

The In-Your-Face Basketball Book

(with Chuck Wielgus)

Raw Recruits

(with Armen Keteyian)

Big Game, Small World:

A Basketball Adventure

White House butler Van Everett pumps
up basketballs in the Outer Oval Office.
(Pete Souza/The White House.)

ALEXANDER WOLFF

THE AUDACITY

OF HOOP

········
Basketball
and the
Age of Obama
········

TEMPLE UNIVERSITY PRESS 〔T〕 *Philadelphia* · *Rome* · *Tokyo*

TEMPLE UNIVERSITY PRESS
Philadelphia, Pennsylvania 19122
www.temple.edu/tempress

Photo editing: Kate Patterson
Research: Damon Hatheway
Interior design: Kate Nichols

Library of Congress Cataloging-in-Publication Data

Wolff, Alexander, 1957–
  The audacity of hoop : basketball and the age of Obama / Alexander Wolff.
    pages cm
  Includes bibliographical references and index.
  ISBN 978-1-4399-1309-3 (hardback : alk. paper)
  1. Obama, Barack.   2. Obama, Barack—Influence.   3. Basketball—United
States.   4. Basketball—Social aspects—United States.   I. Title.
  E908.3.W64 2015
  973.932—dc23
                                                                    2015013672

Printed in the United States of America

9 8 7 6 5 4 3 2 1

FOR CHUCK

who doesn't always like his policies,

but likes the guy—

and like the guy, loves the game

President Obama shoots at the south end of the White House basketball court, converted from a tennis court by the National Park Service in 2009. Personal aide Reggie Love is at right. (Pete Souza/The White House.)

CONTENTS

1 Basketball Jones 1

2 Hoop Dreams from His Father 17
Gaming the President Out 28 • The First Brother-in-Law 31

3 Running Game 35
"The Little Brother I Never Had" 46 • Obama, One-on-One 49
• Players' Choice 51

4 Power, Forward 55
Baracketology 75 • Hardwood Cabinet 77 • The Secretary
of Schoolin' People 85 • Center Circles 89 • Lip Service 90
• Ding-Dong Diplomacy 93 • The World's Most Elegant Locker Room 97
• The Loyal Opposition 104 • The Inevitability of Golf 107

5 The Game in the Age of Obama 111
Shooting the First Shooter 123

Timeline 126

Acknowledgments 149
Notes 151
Selected Bibliography 173
Index 175

At the end of a session of shooting hoops late on an October afternoon in 2010, Obama flips the ball up so it catches a shaft of low-angling light. (Pete Souza/The White House.)

BASKETBALL 1 JONES

The same path had been followed before: ancestry in Kansas, influences from Africa, a high point in Michael Jordan's Chicago, eventual acclamation by the world. And while basketball itself didn't take up residence in the White House in January 2009, the game nonetheless played an outsized role in forming the man who did. As Barack Obama's brother-in-law, Craig Robinson, watched it happen, Robinson came to understand why Obama would become the forty-fourth president of the United States. Basketball, the coach and former college star declared, was why "he's sitting where he's sitting."

The game provided space for young Barry Obama to explore his identity, to wage what he called a "fitful interior struggle . . . to raise myself to be a black man in America." He won a reputation as a cool head and consensus builder while playing informally during college and law school.

In Chicago, basketball helped him connect with both the South Siders he worked with as a community organizer and the circle of professionals who would help launch his political career. A pickup game with Robinson did nothing less than confirm Obama as a worthy suitor to his wife-to-be, Michelle.

On the stump he used basketball to help introduce himself to voters. To the superstitious candidate and his aides, playing ball on election days during the 2008 campaign delivered victories, and failure to play accounted for defeats. The two reddest states Obama flipped in that election, Indiana and North Carolina, each narrowly chose him after he made a basketball lover's case to basketball-loving people. And once he settled into 1600 Pennsylvania Avenue, the game became a touchstone in his exercise of the power of the presidency. Whether demonstrating his Everyman bona fides by announcing his NCAA tournament picks on ESPN or invoking the NBA to project American soft power with gestures of public diplomacy, Obama would pull the game from his toolbox, using it more often and more effectively than any previous president had used any sport.

(Pete Souza/The White House.)

To be sure, many of Obama's presidential predecessors had been athletes, some of them good ones, happy to be identified with their games of choice and ready to wade into the sports debates of the day. Teddy Roosevelt boxed and rode and decried violence in college football. Gerald Ford, errant tee shots and ridicule from *Saturday Night Live* notwithstanding, won two national titles as a lineman at Michigan, where his number is retired. Several commanders in chief installed sporting venues on the White House grounds—Harry Truman's horseshoe pit, Richard Nixon's bowling alley, and George W. Bush's T-ball diamond all served as precedents for Obama's adaptation of the South Lawn tennis court into a full basketball court. Still other chief executives were closely identified with a single sport: Dwight Eisenhower squeezed in eight hundred rounds of golf during two terms and left cleat marks in the floorboards of the Oval Office, while Nixon suggested plays to Washington Redskins coach George Allen. And a couple of southern Democrats preceded Obama as presidents who gave basketball an enthusiastic embrace. Arkansas Razorbacks fan Bill Clinton, who once swung by Harlem's Rucker Park to catch a summer-league game, claimed to have dunked in church-league play as a sixteen-year-old; Jimmy Carter played junior-college ball at Georgia Southwestern in Americus and could trace his passion for the Atlanta Hawks back to a time the networks refused to broadcast the NBA Finals live.

But other than golf to Ike, no game has been as tightly lashed to a president as basketball to Obama. Nor has any president been so enduringly engaged as both player and follower of so strenuous a sport—certainly no team sport. (Herbert Hoover's gatherings of government officials and

In the Oval Office in February 2013, with Samantha Power, a former high school player; her husband, Cass Sunstein; their children; and James Bourke and Veronica Delany, Obama tosses a ball. Later that year Obama would name Power U.S. ambassador to the United Nations. (Pete Souza/The White House.)

journalists for morning tosses of a medicine ball over a volleyball net on the South Lawn do not count as participation in a strenuous team sport.) Obama's chief rival as the most sporting modern president is probably John F. Kennedy. A friend, whom JFK called his "Undersecretary of Baseball," kept him updated on that game, and another member of Kennedy's inner circle assessed the touch football at the family's Hyannis Port compound thusly: "It's touch, but it's murder." Indeed, Kennedy was something of an Obama forerunner—a vigorous Democrat whose rhetorical skills, young family, and zest for the competitive arena signaled a break with the past.

During his first presidential campaign, Obama offered the public a kind of racial Rorschach test. Many whites regarded him as a redemptive figure, someone who could help them and the country move beyond a shameful chapter from the past. Others, including many African Americans, saw a tribune of history. During the 2008–2009 transition, when Obama paid for his order during a visit to Ben's Chili Bowl, an institution in black D.C., the cashier asked him if he wanted change. "Nah, we

(Pete Souza/The White House.)

straight," the president-elect replied—a comment recorded by the flummoxed pool reporter on the scene as, "No, we're straight." That anecdote finds vindication in data: According to the Pew Research Center, most blacks described Obama as "black"; most whites called him "mixed race."

On his 2010 census form, Obama could have checked "white" or "black" or both—and chose to check "black." It's much the same choice he made years ago, playing in places like the basketball court near his grandparents' Honolulu apartment, where he began to develop what he called "an overtly black game." Even as Obama edged into his fifties, the schoolyard provenance of his basketball style could be seen in a fake right, go left crossover dribble and a double-clutch pull-up jumper in the lane (see "Gaming the President Out," page 28). But as he aged, and after falling in with a circle of pickup buddies who had played formally at Division III colleges and in the Ivy League, his game seemed also to nod at the heritage of his mother, whose own parents came from small-town Kansas. In the same way that his political career obviated much of the received wisdom about race, Obama's game made a muddle of rigid racial categories.

Basketball insiders don't flinch at identifying black players who "play white" (Paul Silas, Quinn Buckner, Charles Oakley) or white players who "play black" (Billy Cunningham, Rex Chapman, Jason Williams). The "plays white/plays black" parlor game becomes even more fascinating

Facing page: Regulars in presidential pickup games included Secretary of Education Arne Duncan (*left*), a former star at Harvard, and the president's personal aide, Reggie Love, a member of Duke's 2001 NCAA title team, being challenged here by Obama for the ball. (Pete Souza/The White House.)

Basketball
Jones

5

when persona is factored in along with playing style. "[In Obama] you have a laced-up professional off the court, a 'white' persona, who throws behind-the-back passes and busts crossovers on the court," said Claude Johnson, who in 2008 founded Baller-in-Chief.com, a website devoted to Obama and basketball. "Persona-wise, you'd think he'd have a basically stiff game, like Tim Duncan's. But no—he's showing up at a North Carolina practice, and he's playing ball with [NBA guard Chris] Duhon. So the guy on the street says, 'Whoa, he's got a little *game!*'"

More than that, Obama had long ago adopted the carriage of a ballplayer to go with the shots and moves. It was part of what made him, in the phrase of poet Ishmael Reed, "the President of the Cool." *Slam,* the arbiter of the asphalt game, likened the Obama gait to that of Julius Erving, the player whose soaring silhouette had graced the poster that hung on young Barry's bedroom wall. As the magazine put it, "Not a stereotype, Obama's an archetype."

(Pete Souza/The White House.)

During a remote broadcast from NBA All-Star Weekend in 2009, CNN's John King gathered a handful of current and former NBA players around a set to screen for them video of Obama playing ball. After airing a clip of the candidate from the previous July, sinking a three-pointer in front of a rolling minicam during a visit to U.S. troops in Kuwait, King asked Steve Nash of the Phoenix Suns whether Obama should have shown more swagger after making the shot.

"No," Nash replied, faintly irritated that King didn't understand where cool comes from. "He's got plenty of swagger."

In a passage from *Dreams from My Father,* his 1995 memoir, Obama captured the essence of the game, with its staccato cadences and continuous action: "And something else, too, something nobody talked about: a way of being together when the game was tight and the sweat broke and the best players stopped worrying about their points and the worst players got swept up in the moment and the score only mattered because that's how you sustained the trance. In the middle of which you might make a move or a pass that surprised even you, so that even the guy guarding you had to smile, as if to say, 'Damn . . .'"

If a presidential campaign is an MRI of the soul, as Obama advisor and strategist David Axelrod liked to say, a pickup game can administer a kind of polygraph of the heart. Obama's experience with organized basketball included three high school seasons at Honolulu's Punahou School, only one on the "A" varsity, and that spent largely on the bench. For years he nursed resentments over having played such a bit part, blaming conflict between his self-taught style and the buttoned-up expectations of coach Chris McLachlin. During their senior season Obama led a delegation of pine riders to the coach's office to argue for

During his Chicago Bulls' swing through Washington in February 2009, Obama engages Wizards fan Miles Rawls in some friendly trash talk, including Rawls's advice, with the home team comfortably ahead: "Warm up the limo, Sir, because this is a wrap." Here Obama gives Rawls, the longtime P.A. man at D.C.'s Goodman Summer League, epidermal credit where it's due after the Wizards' JaVale McGee flushes an alley-oop. (Photo by Preston Keres/*The Washington Post*/Getty Images.)

Obama greets the defending NBA Champions, the Los Angeles Lakers, in the Green Room of the White House in January 2010. *From left:* Didier Ilunga-Mbenga, Pau Gasol, and Andrew Bynum. (Pete Souza/The White House.)

more playing time. "I reminded him it wasn't about him," McLachlin said. "It was about the team."

The disappointment of his high-school experience ensured that, later in life, Obama would be less a retired ballplayer trying to keep in shape than a "baller" with an unrequited love. There was meaning, Claude Johnson believed, in Obama's being more a product of basketball's speakeasies than its licensed establishments. "If he'd [continued] in organized ball, it's very possible he'd have gotten the whole thing out of his system. . . . There's pathos there. You're still trying to prove you're good enough to start on your high school team, even if you really did get over it. In basketball you're continually trying to prove yourself, and in pickup even more so, because there is no record. You can't say, 'Oh, I'm 19–1.' It's all on you."

Pickup ballplayers don't converse as much as golfers do during a round. But they get just as quickly to judgments about personality and, in contrast to golf, can explore virtues like collaborative aptitude. There's also the temperament that ballers learn to bring to the court, if only to make sure—this is Obama again, writing in *Dreams*—that no one can "sneak up behind you to see emotions, like hurt or fear, that you didn't want them to see." Asked the boxers-versus-briefs question, obligatory in presidential campaigns ever since Clinton answered it in 1992, Obama came up with the pitch-perfect pickup ballplayer's reply: "I

(Pete Souza/The White House.)

don't answer those humiliating questions, but whichever one it is, I look good in 'em."

Organized basketball, particularly in high school, is an exercise in submission to a system of command and control. Pickup ball, by contrast, entails collective governance and ongoing conflict resolution, even as all parties want and expect some measurable sorting of winners from losers. Pickup, to turn on their head the unworthy words of 2008 GOP vice presidential candidate Sarah Palin, is community organizing in which everyone has "actual responsibilities."

Pickup ball is rife with moments that call for the skill set of the politician. Positioning oneself to call next, setting up another player so the favor might be returned, soothing the temper and ego that can be as confounding in one's own teammate as in an opponent—these are all negotiations, "going to conference" by another name, a process that would break down if not for participants who, like Obama, traffic in conciliation. A functional pickup game needs a quorum of players who can metaphorically, as Obama did literally, carry both Indiana and Vermont.

For all its associations with the inner city, pickup ball by the time Obama took the oath of office had become a universal American pastime. His political opponents might insinuate that the playground game, and by extension Obama, was too urban, or alien to white America. But with three-on-three tournaments like Gus Macker and Hoop-It-Up well established in small towns and red states, and FIBA, the game's international federation, on the verge of winning a berth for three-on-three in the Olympics, the informal game had gone mainstream. Indeed, pickup ball evoked a time that Americans of a certain age, urban and suburban, black and white, looked back on with nostalgia—when kids weren't stashed with third parties or chauffeured to play-dates but made their way on their own to the playground or park, where they chose teams, shot fingers, and, like Obama, grew up along the way.

"There's an ethical undertone in pickup that people miss," Craig Robinson said after the 2008 election. "The game has to be played fairly or it breaks down. You practice an honor code, making your own calls and giving them up. If Barack walks, he'll give it up, not sneak it by you. You play with hundreds of guys who'd never do that. It all gets back to how you can tell a guy's character on the court. And it's an indicator of how he ran his campaign. You can't keep all those plates spinning if you're not telling the truth."

(Pete Souza/The White House.)

Barack Obama is a Baby Boomer by any definition of the term. Born in 1961, he's part of the great spike in the American birthrate between the end of World War II and 1965, which produced the cohort that, as he served his two terms in the White House, sat heavily astride the American demographic. Yet cultural critics have come to subdivide Boomers into two camps: members of the Woodstock Generation, who actually partook of the sixties, and younger Boomers like Obama, born after 1953, whose experience tended to be quite different.

Author Jonathan Pontell calls this latter group Generation Jones. Overshadowed by those older brothers and sisters on whom the popular culture dotes, Jonesers tend to be Smith-and-Jones anonymous. As they benchmarked themselves against those a decade or so ahead of them, many late Boomers felt an urge to "keep up with the Joneses," which in turn stoked a competitiveness that isn't usually associated with the spirit of the counterculture. And while the typical Joneser grew up with high hopes for achievement and prosperity, many made their way through adulthood nagged by a sense that they had somehow failed to fulfill their promise, which left them with an unrequited yearning, or "jonesing," for something more.

Personally and politically, Obama embodied many of these traits. He rejected easy sixties shibboleths. Abandoned by his father and left behind for long stretches by his mother, an anthropologist who studied Asian cultures, he felt anything but fussed over. Though it took its time to kick in, there would be no mistaking his competitiveness and striver's desire to prove his worth. Even if the polarized politics during his presidency tended to

Obama cools down after playing pickup ball in Los Angeles in May 2012. Seated in chairs (*from left*) are actors Don Cheadle, Tobey Maguire, and George Clooney. Friends of Clooney's, including WWE diva and actress Stacy Keibler, are also pictured. (Pete Souza/The White House.)

obscure it, Obama had a conciliatory nature, precisely what you'd expect of someone who sat between the idealism of the Woodstock Generation and the cynicism of Generation X.

Moreover, Boomers were the first cohort in which men, even into their fifties and sixties, used unorganized basketball not simply as a schoolyard pastime or ethnic marker but also as a means of regular exercise, socializing, and bonding. (A photo like the one on page 11, of the president cooling off after playing with actors Don Cheadle, Tobey Maguire, and George Clooney, could not have been taken thirty or forty years earlier. Its forerunner is a shot of Gerald Ford with Jackie Gleason and Bob Hope, teeing it up at Gleason's Inverrary Classic.) The vogue in pickup basketball was driven as much by economic and cultural forces as generational ones. Drawing a contrast with agrarian baseball and industrial football, academic Michael Mandelbaum calls basketball "the hallmark game of the post-industrial age." Basketball, to apply a postindustrial phrase, is a net-

(Pete Souza/The White House.)

worked sport, with pickup ball a social network of sorts—one that, in Obama's case, according to his half-sister, Maya Soetoro-Ng, supplied the president with "constancy and kinship with friends, a way to recline into his past."

But a network can be more than a structure imposed from without. Basketball ran unbroken from Obama's fractured beginnings through the circles and circumstances he

came across in young adulthood and later life. The game, in the words of his biographer, David Maraniss, "connected the disconnected parts of him."

Shortly after Obama was elected, John Rogers, Craig Robinson's old Princeton teammate, provided interim offices for the presidential transition team at his Chicago investment firm. Until a suite could be readied in the Federal Building downtown, the president-elect called world leaders from a conference room named after Rogers and Robinson's college coach, the high priest of ball control, Pete Carril. Obama must have been bemused by the irony: The undomesticated high school ballplayer had fallen in with Robinson, Rogers, and former Harvard captain and future secretary of education Arne Duncan, who together won multiple national three-on-three titles, schooling players half their age by bringing smarts and structure to the playground game. "He's around a lot of guys who know how to play," Rogers said, "and aren't just running up and down the court."

But that evolution shouldn't have come as a surprise. Study his life and career, and you'll recognize in Obama a pattern of counterweight—of drifting toward yin when there's yang, and vice versa. At Punahou, with order and

The president checks in with the Georgetown student section in January 2010 at Washington's Verizon Center before the Hoyas' defeat of Duke. During the second half Obama spent several minutes on-air with CBS announcers Verne Lundquist and Clark Kellogg calling a layup off a spin move. (Pete Souza/The White House.)

Clockwise from upper left: Obama embraces Bill Russell before the unveiling of a statue of the former Celtics star in Boston's City Hall Plaza; the First Coach gets shots up with daughters Malia (*left*) and Sasha; Obama blocks a shot by personal aide Reggie Love in the gym at St. Bart's Church in Manhattan; former NBA center Dikembe Mutombo fills the doorframe as he prepares to leave the Oval Office. (Pete Souza/The White House.)

orthodoxy around him, he chose to develop a gutbucket game. On Chicago's South Side, where both basketball and life tended toward entropy, he literally worked as an organizer. On a Harvard Law School campus split into ideological camps, he was a difference-splitter. The man whose half-sister recognized in him equal parts their mother's idealism and grandmother's pragmatism seemed to be drawn naturally to dialectics. Indeed, a riddle sits at the heart of basketball, whose appeal to him, Obama said, lay in an "improvisation within a discipline that I find very powerful." With its serial returns to equilibrium—cut backdoor against an overplay; shoot when the defense sags—the game represents Obama's intellectual nature come alive.

Another dialectic, old as the ancients, poses the great challenge of government: how best to balance the rights of the individual with the welfare of the group. It's a tension that surfaced in Obama's speeches and writings again and again. "Our individualism has always been bound by a set of communal values, the glue upon which every healthy society depends," he wrote in *The Audacity of Hope*. In the Africa of his paternal roots, he had

(Pete Souza/The White House.)

watched the pendulum swing so far toward the collective that the individual could be overburdened and paralyzed. In the America he led, he saw the elite gaming a financial system so enfeebled that the collective was left to shoulder the worst effects of deficits and recession. Where was the golden mean, that place where We the People could find "a way of being together" where *the best players stopped worrying about their points and the worst players got swept up in the moment and the score only mattered because that's how you sustained the trance*?

Such is the tension at the heart of hoop. Titles await teams that can intertwine what Obama, speaking of America, once called "these twin strands—the individualistic and the communal, autonomy and solidarity." Maybe Obama needed to be a Punahou reserve to recognize that truth and become a Hawaii state champion. In much the same way, being a community organizer probably helped him become a U.S. senator. And perhaps Americans twice chose him as their president because they too had come to recognize that, in the end, it wasn't about you, it was about the team.

December 1971 is the last time Barry Obama will see his father, who gives him a basketball as a Christmas gift. (Courtesy of The White House.)

HOOP DREAMS FROM HIS FATHER

Barack Obama's father, a Kenyan exchange student at the University of Hawaii, abandoned his wife and son soon after young Barack's birth in 1961. Ann Dunham was left to raise Barry first in Honolulu and then in Indonesia, where she moved in 1967 after remarriage to another exchange student, Lolo Soetoro. Four years later Ann sent her boy back to Hawaii to live with her parents, who arranged for him to attend Punahou, the elite private school to which he won a scholarship. There he began to construct for himself an identity as "a black man in America," even if, as he has written, "beyond the given of my appearance, no one around me seemed to know exactly what that meant."

Aside from African Americans stationed with the military, Hawaii in the seventies could count barely four hundred black residents. Two events conspired to help Obama address his alienation. In December

1971, during a visit that would become ten-year-old Barry's only memory of his father, Barack Sr. gave him a basketball for Christmas. There's no accounting for exactly why a native of a country where the game was hardly played chose this particular present, but Barry would come to regard that basketball as a charge as much as a gift.

The second episode would take place several weeks later, after Barry's grandfather scored two scarce tickets to a University of Hawaii game. Top-class basketball had never before taken root in the islands, but between 1970 and 1972 the Rainbows' "Fabulous Five" put together a 47–8 record and delivered the school's first NIT and NCAA bids. With aloha-print shorts and bountiful Afros, junior-college transfers Al Davis, Jerome (Hook) Freeman, Dwight Holiday, and Bob Nash, joined by John Penebacker, an Air Force vet discovered in a local Armed Forces league, averaged more than ninety points a game as the pep band played *Jesus Christ Superstar*

(Courtesy of Punahou School.)

and fans spilled raucously into the aisles. In his autobiography Obama recorded his impressions of the game: "I had watched the players in warm-ups, still boys themselves but to me poised and confident warriors, chuckling to each other about some inside joke, glancing over the heads of fawning fans to wink at the girls on the sidelines, casually flipping layups or tossing high-arcing jumpers until the whistle blew and the centers jumped and the players joined in furious battle."

This, he decided, was a world into which he wanted to fit his young self. Soon he began to haunt a nearby playground, where his grandmother watched him from her bedroom window ten stories up. By the time he hit his teens, he was taking his ball to school, getting up shots between classes and over lunch hour. Only years later, in the midst of writing *Dreams from My Father,* did he recognize a basketball life launched with his father's gift: "I hadn't even remembered that until I wrote the book. But then I thought to myself, Wow, there's so much there. Him giving me the ball, him finally showing up in my life, the connection of the African-American community and identity: All that stuff gets wrapped up and it becomes very important to me."

Chris McLachlin, the varsity coach, remembered Barry crossing the Punahou campus, books in one hand and a ball bouncing from the other, and couldn't recall a player of his who loved the game more. Teachers and students remarked on his stride, the suppleness afoot that the world would eventually see in a candidate and president who bounded up to a stage or down to a tarmac. As he improved and grew more confident, Obama would drift down to the school's lower courts, sometimes even after basketball practice. There—and at the university gym and playgrounds around town—he would engage the island's best adult players as they ran full-court into the tropical evenings.

In those pickup games, Obama has written, "a handful of black men, mostly gym rats and has-beens, would teach me an attitude that didn't just have to do with the sport. That respect came from what you did and not who your daddy was. That you could talk stuff to rattle an opponent, but that you should shut the hell up if you couldn't back it up." An airy civility prevails in Hawaii, a corollary of the "aloha spirit," which lends the local pidgin idioms like "no talk stink" and "cool head, main thing." The playground served up attitude and argot with a harder edge, more main-land than island, and that suited Barry just fine.

To some extent, Obama admitted, he was "living out a caricature of black male adolescence" with his enthusiasm for the game. An African American senior at Punahou who hoped to become an attorney watched as Obama, then two years younger, inscribed a parting message in the graduate's yearbook: *Get that law degree, and someday you can help me sue my NBA team for more money.* But even if Obama played "with a consuming passion that would always exceed my limited talent," as he would write, that consumption came with a perk: "At least on the basketball court I could find a community of sorts, with an inner life all its own. It was there that I would make my closest white friends, on turf where blackness couldn't be a disadvantage."

That poster of Julius Erving—a black man with whom kids of any race would have happily traded places—is a

(Courtesy of Punahou School.)

totem of how the seventies delivered a generation of white adolescents who, for reasons of sports or music or style, on some level wished they were black. Obama represented a variation on the theme: a black kid who, in a peculiar way, also wished he were black. But in his case the stakes were higher. "To this day he still thinks about how hard that time was," said his brother-in-law, Craig Robinson. "And how'd he get through it? With a basketball."

During all those hours of play Obama developed his "overtly black game." A favorite song, William DeVaughn's "Be Thankful for What You've Got," is a mid-seventies ode to inner-city pose-striking, with its invocation of *Diggin' the scene / With a gangsta lean,* and Obama's obsession with basketball was indeed a kind of pose. "There were some issues of racial identity that played themselves out on the basketball court," he has admitted.

Eventually he would have to apply the message in the title of that song to his experience as a member of the Punahou Buff 'n' Blue. After playing jayvee as a sophomore and making the second varsity the following season, Obama ascended to McLachlin's top varsity as a senior. (Punahou fielded multiple teams in some sports to accommodate its large enrollment.) There, Obama recalled, "we had some con-flict. Some tension." He made his pitch for more playing time. And he listened to a black friend suggest that he now featured in that hoary and tragic African American basketball narrative: Black Prometheus, straitjacketed by The Man.

Nearly three decades later Obama could see it all more objectively. "Especially in high school, I thought I was better than I was," he said. "In retrospect, I don't blame the coach. But at the time I was sure that he was biased against me. . . . I don't think it was racial; I thought he just didn't like me, didn't respect my game.

"In retrospect I'd say it was more my fault than his. I was an undisciplined player. I came to the game late. This is where probably not having a dad or somebody to structure my game in some ways made a difference. I never developed a right hand. I never did drills or practiced, so I wasn't getting many minutes my senior year. I probably ended up having more fun playing playground."

From McLachlin's perspective, it was simple: "He was really, really good and could have started for any other team in the state. But *we* were really good, and it was so hard to break into that group. Three kids went on to Division I scholarships, two at his position. [One of those three, John Kamana, played in the NFL.] He was an independent thinker and kind of an independent player. But despite the fact that there was pushback, he never lost sight of what the goal was. We sometimes don't get the lessons teachers teach us until years later."

McLachlin, then in his early thirties, eventually came

(Courtesy of The White House.)

to believe that Obama would have had a more rewarding experience if the two had met up later in his career. "I would have made a place for a player like him," he said. "But in those early days I was much more conventional. Play five, maybe one or two subs, go to the bench with a big lead. What he got is what he got. Obviously it was frustrating for him not to get as much time as he thought he deserved. But the end result was that we had a pretty amazing year."

The Punahou team that beat Moanalua High by thirty-two points for the 1979 state title is regarded as one of the greatest in Hawaii history. Obama missed a free throw and scored on a garbage-time breakaway that day. During his senior season, Obama would later say, "[I learned about] being part of something and finishing it up. And I learned a lot about discipline, about handling disappointments, about being more team-oriented and realizing that not everything is about you."

In 2004, as a U.S. senator from Illinois, Obama returned to Punahou to address a packed chapel. From the dais, the old second-stringer admitted to having been "kind of a pain in the butt when I was here." Then he caught a glimpse of McLachlin in the shadows. "Coach Mac, is that you?" he said. "I've gotta tell you something. I really wasn't as good as I thought I was."

McLachlin felt a weight leave his shoulders. "As much as I berate myself for my own lack of maturity as a coach at

Obama (*upper row, far right*), who saw only spot duty for Punahou's 1979 Hawaii state title team, at one point joined several teammates to lobby coach Chris McLachlin (*front, center*) for more playing time. (Courtesy of Punahou School.)

WE GO PLAY HOOP

Thanks Tut, Gramps, Choom Gang, and Ray for all the good times.

Barry Obama

(Courtesy of Punahou School.)

that time, obviously some stuff stuck with him and helped shape his character," he said. "I didn't screw him up, is what I mean. I'm relieved that I didn't quash his passion. It can be painful for a kid who doesn't play."

Obama has alluded to the many hours he devoted to basketball as time he might have spent rounding himself out. "I had bought into a set of false assumptions about what it means to be black," he confessed. The game had nonetheless dug its hooks in him. By the time he left Punahou, Obama knew how to get lost in a book, discuss geopolitics with friends, and write something up for the literary magazine. Indeed, clique-conscious classmates could never figure out if Barry wanted to be a jock or a brain. But one phrase leaped from his senior yearbook page. It was an epigraph for his coming of age in Hawaii: "We go play hoop."

As Obama made his fitful way after high school, basketball abided. He spent two years at Occidental, a liberal arts college in Los Angeles with an enrollment smaller than Punahou's. That first fall he worked out informally with fifteen or so freshman hopefuls, many of whom would, after he emerged as a national political figure, recall him and his stylish game. One remembered that, in an era of over-the-calf tube socks, Obama seemed to make a point of wearing Peds. Though he apparently never joined the team, he continued to play "noonball" with faculty, staff, and other students. As Eric Newhall, an English professor and regular in those games, later put it, "The greatest contribution Occidental has made to American democracy was to help Barack Obama decide that his future wasn't in basketball."

By sophomore year Obama had thrown himself into classwork and anti-apartheid activism and begun to map a path east. "What I needed was a community, I realized, a community that cut deeper than the common despair that black friends and I shared when reading the latest crime statistics, or the high fives I might exchange on the basketball court," he wrote. "A place where I could put down stakes and test my commitments." He transferred to Columbia and became more serious about his future. But he still made basketball pilgrimages to Harlem, "to play on courts I'd once read about."

After graduation he took that community organizing position on Chicago's South Side, where he was tasked with bringing together white priests, black pastors, civic leaders, and ordinary people to solve common problems. He used the game as a means to get through to an on-the-edge adolescent already scaling back his expectations for life. But organizing proved to be frustrating work marked by only intermittent victories, and after four years Obama decided that to effect real change, he needed better credentials.

In 1988 he enrolled at Harvard Law School and quickly found his way into games that went off late afternoons at "the MAC," the undergraduate Malkin Athletic Center, as well as argument-studded affairs in the Law School's old Hemenway Gym, with its dim light and creaky floor. While playing ball, Obama met Eric Whitaker, a medical resident at Harvard who, after Obama's return to Chicago, would become a close friend. And he joined a delegation of the Black Law Students Association for a game at a maximum-security prison in Walpole, Massachusetts, where inmates lining the court made sure the visitors knew how many cigarettes rode on the outcome. "He made the mistake of asking the guy who was guarding him, 'What are you in for?'" recalled classmate Hill Harper, a future star of *CSI: NY*, who organized the game as an outreach exercise. "The brother said 'double murder,' and Barack didn't take another shot. That just goes to show you his good judgment. Even then."

When he became the first African American elected to head the *Harvard Law Review*, Obama won a nineteenth

ballot victory largely because members of the staff's conservative faction believed he would give them a fair hearing. By then many fellow students had taken his measure on the court. "He was a passer despite the fact he could score," remembered classmate Andrew Feldstein. "'Inclusive' is the best way to describe him. Some people who play pickup ball lose the sense that it's pickup, but he never did."

Hemenway Gym sat adjacent to Gannett House, site of the offices of the *Review,* so Obama could shuttle between the two, afternoons and evenings. "It was law school, so you didn't look at the clock," remembered classmate Julius Genachowski, who would become Obama's first Federal Communications Commission chairman. Genachowski recalled Obama once appearing at the *Review* with a bandage on a broken nose just suffered during a game.

In 1989 Obama began a second tour of Chicago, now as a summer associate with the law firm of Sidley Austin. There he met and would eventually begin dating an attorney named Michelle Robinson. But before their relationship could advance too far, Michelle had a test to administer. Her new beau claimed to play a little ball, and growing up, she had heard her father, Fraser, and brother, Craig, a two-time Ivy Player of the Year at Princeton, insist that character is revealed on the court. So she hatched a plan. "Phone calls were made," recalled her brother, who rounded up a quorum of friends. "I didn't want the game to be

. . . .

On Chicago's South Side in 1995, Obama takes a break from collecting signatures on nominating petitions for his first run for office. He won an Illinois State Senate seat the following November. (Copyright © Marc PoKempner, 1995.)

too intimidating, so it wouldn't be too painful for me" in case he had to tell his sister that the boyfriend with the odd name hadn't made the grade. Robinson didn't have to worry. Years later, in campaign appearances on Obama's behalf, he would retell the story, with a kicker: If I could trust him with my sister, you can trust him with your vote.

Through the Robinsons, Obama joined a circle of ballplayers that foreshadowed the cast he would run with during his time in the White House (see "Hardwood Cabinet," page 77). And the sport introduced him to some of the Chicagoans who would provide the counsel and cash that launched his political career. Hyatt Hotels heiress Penny Pritzker, who would serve as Obama's national campaign finance chair before becoming secretary of commerce, enrolled her children in a youth basketball program in which Craig Robinson coached. John Rogers of Ariel Investments had captained the Princeton team during Robinson's freshman season. A buddy of Rogers and Robinson's, a parking garage baron named Marty Nesbitt, would become one of Obama's closest friends. Perhaps the best ballplayer of the lot, former Harvard captain Arne Duncan, eventually left his position as chief of the Chicago public schools to become Obama's secretary of education. To men in the neighborhoods of Hyde Park and Kenwood, where the Obamas and many of their friends lived, pickup ball served the social function of golf, with a younger, hipper edge. "I saw a lot earlier what the nation would come to understand—that, yes, he has a nice smile and can string words together, but he's also a killer," said Duncan. "He's not out there just to get some exercise and take some shots."

Obama would often leave that tight basketball circle to dissolve into the hoop crowd. During the late nineties, when he spent four years as a lecturer at the University of Chicago Law School, he turned up regularly at the Henry Crown Fieldhouse on campus. One undergraduate in those games was Tucker Max, who would go on to recount drunken exploits and sexual conquests in books like *I Hope They Serve Beer in Hell* and *Assholes Finish First*. Decades later Max shared his impressions of Obama the ballplayer for a dinner date: "He never really complained about anything—like when other people called borderline fouls for instance—unless it was an obvious wrong call, then he would say something. But only like a reproachful father. Not an arguer at all, and he was always nice, even when he was correcting you. He never made you feel bad about yourself or anything like that. He was always a very nice, sincere guy, to everyone.

"If there was some conflict on the court, over a foul called or ball out of bounds or something like that, he was always a voice of calm and reason. He was an adult before he was a basketball player. . . . I can't ever remember him rattled, like some of the other professors would get."

"Um," Max's companion replied, "you just described his presidency."

During those games at the University of Chicago, the future president sometimes found himself on the court with a Nobel laureate, or a homeless man, or a self-avowed asshole like Max, or Duncan's mother, Sue, who took part into her sixties and had such a reputation for physical play that, years later, Obama would laughingly take up old grievances with her son. "Status, prestige—all that stuff got thrown out the window," said Arne Duncan of those games at the Fieldhouse. "The rule was 'winner stays on,' so if you wanted to play, you had to win. The Ivory Tower didn't extend to the court."

In 2011 and 2012, after following the president over the course of six months, *Vanity Fair*'s Michael Lewis found vestiges of those associations in what he described as Obama's radical common touch. Basketball, Lewis suggested, was both a root cause of and a staging ground for this characteristic: "His desire to hear out junior people is a warm personality trait as much as a cool tactic, of a piece with his desire to play golf with White House cooks rather than with CEOs and basketball with people who treat him as just another player on the court. . . . The man has his status needs, but they are unusual. And he has a tendency, an unthinking first step, to subvert established status structures."

Anyone who plays basketball has "an unthinking first step." It begins to get at who we really are. And if we're lucky, it also indicates the better angels of our nature.

Gaming the President Out

The Rosetta Stone to Barack Obama's playing style is a two-minute highlight reel on YouTube. Three-fourths of the way through his presidency, *The Barack Obama Basketball Mixtape,* with clips going back to the 1979 Hawaii state title game, had been viewed almost 700,000 times. The film depicted someone whose game might be described as Old School Schoolyard—"a little stiff," *Slam* magazine called it, "but contextually spry." Or as Shane Battier, who played at Obama's forty-ninth birthday party in 2010, put it: "Fairly good quicks . . . pretty good handle . . . awkward, janky."

The earliest footage vindicated Obama's claim, "I could get to the rim on anybody." Later clips showed a more earthbound player, one his brother-in-law Craig Robinson described as "extremely lefthanded." Even as an aging ballplayer, Obama showcased baseline drives, double-

(*Outdoor shots in this section*: Pete Souza/The White House.)

pumps in the lane, and mambo off the dribble. He also shot a midrange jumper with fairly consistent form, even if his high school nickname, Barry O'Bomber, was always a misnomer. After watching video of the president-elect, Magic Johnson declared that Obama thought like a point guard, rarely following his passes: "Most YMCA players, they follow the ball. They pass and want it right back."

Asked to nominate someone Obama's game reminded them of, people who had seen him play tended to tick off the names of guards and lefties: Manu Ginobili, Tony Parker, Dick Barnett, Jamal Crawford, Lionel Hollins, Dennis Johnson, Kenny Anderson, Delonte West. Invoking size, savvy, left-handedness, and self-possession, Robinson named as a play-alike Lenny Wilkens, the Hall of Famer who campaigned for Obama and whose autograph graced the basketball that decorated the president-elect's spare Chicago transition office. "Lenny was a thicker player and Barack is very slight, even if [defensive] physicality doesn't bother him," Robinson said. "But the calmness of Lenny Wilkens's game,

that's Barack. He knows the game well enough to fit in, and doesn't appear to be out of his element athletically."

Even as Washington Wizards G.M. Ernie Grunfeld described the president as "a solid weekend warrior," Obama as he hit his fifties

(Photo by Bill Frakes/*Sports Illustrated*/Getty Images.)

remained something short of the total package. He hadn't dunked since high school. With Barry having given way to Barack, he no longer had a nickname, notwithstanding the efforts of *Chicago Sun-Times* columnist Rick Telander, who suggested one, Bam-Bam, that failed to stick. His usual get-up of black sweatpants and gray

T-shirt—the police academy trainee look—never threatened to set a trend. Telander guessed the reason for the sweatpants: "Bird legs."

"He was not some doofus out there trying to get exercise," recalled Tucker Max, the author who often played with Obama as a student at the University of Chicago, where the future president served as a lecturer during the late nineties. "[But] he didn't have what basketball players call 'old man game.' Basketball players who have that know every trick, use every advantage, and kill your youth and quickness with their guile and strength. That wasn't Barack. He would beat you if given space, but if you played even half-decent defense on him, you could take him out of the game.

"I saw so many people pick him first, and then get burned because he didn't play up to that pick. He was a great third option for your team, though, like a Ron Harper to [Michael] Jordan and [Scottie] Pippen."

Whose game Obama most resembled was very much in the eye of the beholder, and political orientation had a way of coloring

a beholder's eye. A John McCain attack ad during the 2008 campaign meant to draw a comparison to Allen Iverson, "blinged-up, camera-hungry." At the other end of the spectrum, filmmaker Spike Lee wore a T-shirt that featured Obama as an airborne Vince Carter, and McCain as a hapless Frédéric Weis, the 7'2" Frenchman whom Carter had posterized during the 2000 Olympics. Both images offered a thrill at the partisan margins, but each was a caricature. By the end of that campaign, Obama was neither Iverson nor Carter, but someone who had closed the deal with the electorate by selling himself essentially as Wilkens, who for several seasons in Seattle was literally a coach on the floor and in 1979 guided the Sonics to an NBA title exclusively from the bench.

At middle age, Obama's playing style had morphed into something as racially ambiguous as his persona. As Robinson suggested during the 2008 campaign, aging ballplayers tend to play a less flashy, more earthbound "white" game, and Obama was no exception, even if he had throttled back mostly out of self-preservation.

"As I've gotten older," he said in 2007, "I tend to be easier going in the sense that, if I'm not injured, I'm happy."

He also copped to talking trash, although it would usually be more of the "That all ya got?" than the "Yo momma" variety. "Somebody like [personal aide] Reggie [Love] I love talking trash to, somebody who I know is basically better than me," Obama said. "Reggie has pointed it out. . . . 'Nah, you don't want to let Barack win. You'll never hear the end of it.'

"I'll make you feel bad about yourself if we beat you real bad."

Or as Michelle Obama said: "With people who don't know him, he's going to be very gracious. But if he knows you? He can do his share of trash-talking. He and his mother and his sister, Maya, sometimes they'd play Scrabble when his mother was alive, and there was nothing but trash talk. His mother was trash-talking."

One of Obama's protean qualities is an ability to change diction and cadence according to the audience he addresses. In much the same way, he had a knack for taking the measure of whatever pickup situation he found himself in. Playing with most junior aides or voters on the campaign trail, he would defer, making sure to keep the ball moving. But if playing with Love or Arne Duncan on a Saturday morning in D.C., he could shift into a higher gear. "I've seen him make six straight threes, and other times shoot once and not shoot again," said Arthur Jackson, a regular in those games. "His mind is focused on winning. 'Let's see who's hot and get him the ball.'"

Executives do something like this when they synthesize advice from colleagues; a president does it when listening to options around the table in the Situation Room. To play with those better than you is an art—one that Obama, by middle age, had mastered. ∎

The First Brother-in-Law

He introduced his sister, Michelle, to wild cheers at the 2008 Democratic National Convention in Denver. At the inauguration the following January, his scarf of orange and black—the colors of Oregon State, the school where he had just begun his first season as coach—popped from the tableau on the Capitol steps. Craig Robinson played many roles, including a famous turn, one spring Saturday morning in 1990 in a gym on Chicago's South Side, as Barack Obama's judge, jury, and potential executioner.

His sister, Michelle, then twenty-six, had been dating Obama for about a year. Now she leaned on her brother: Could he apply the test that he and their father, Fraser, always talked about—that character reveals itself on the court—and take her suitor balling with his crew, which included past Ivy League captains Arne Duncan, formerly of Harvard, and John Rogers, who had been Robinson's teammate at Princeton?

As it turned out, Obama shot when he had a shot, but not to the point of self-delusion. He passed when he ought to pass, but not so often as to seem like a suck-up to his girlfriend's brother and his friends. These patterns held up over the morning, which was important, for the Robinson men also believed that a tired player regresses to the mean of his true nature. "Confident without being cocky," Robinson reported back. "Your boy is straight, and he can ball."

Obama had some notion of what was going on. "If you're going to play basketball with the older brother of the woman you're dating, the third-leading scorer in Princeton history who was drafted by the Sixers, they're going to be checking out your game," he said in 2007. "That's the assumption."

The trope that basketball reveals character is so hoary and trite that it seems ripped from *McGuffey's Reader,* and to his credit Obama has rejected it as simplistic: "I've known some people who were just jackasses on the court who were good people otherwise. . . . So [basketball] will give you a sliver of it, but people compensate in other parts of their lives."

That morning nonetheless became a cornerstone of the Obama creation myth—"the most important basketball game Robinson has ever

been involved in," as *Esquire*'s Chuck Klosterman put it in 2009. "And it probably always will be, even if the Beavers go to the Final Four."

Robinson never did take Oregon State to the Final Four, or even the NCAA tournament. But in Corvallis he traced a trajectory with parallels to his brother-in-law's in the White House—an auspicious opening, with high hopes eventually running up against reality.

The Beavers hired Robinson after his two seasons at Brown, where he had just led the Bruins to a school-record nineteen wins and second place in the Ivy League, ahead of his alma mater. An offer to take over a 6–25 team that had just gone winless in the Pac-12 wouldn't ordinarily have much appeal. But Brown couldn't offer athletic scholarships. Princeton and Penn had sat atop the Ivies for years, swapping NCAA bids between them. And Robinson didn't lack for confidence. As he told the

Facing page: Craig Robinson spent six seasons on the Oregon State sideline before taking a job at ESPN. Robinson's mother, Marian, sits to the president's left during this November 2009 game at George Washington University. (AP Photo/Gerald Herbert.)

junior senator from Illinois in late 2006, when Obama asked Robinson for his thoughts on a run for the presidency, "I may not be ready for the Kentucky job, but if someone offers it to me, I'm taking it!"

In Corvallis he had the same instant impact as in Providence. While still "trying to sort out the forensics of what happened here," as he put it, Robinson led the Beavers to eighteen wins that first season, including seven in the league. The biggest, a 69–65 victory at first-place California two days after the inauguration, began with a pregame standing ovation from the Obama-friendly Berkeley crowd. The last clinched a postseason title, in the College Basketball Invitational tournament, which elevated the Beavers to .500, their best record in more than a decade. As his sister and brother-in-law settled into the White House and enjoyed a grace period, Robinson refuted the charge that Oregon State wouldn't have hired him if not for his family tie.

After a first season that seemed to defy the laws of physics, Robinson soon found himself subjected to the laws of rising expectations. The Beavers never finished higher than fifth in the Pac-12. By the time Robinson took the stage at the 2012 Democratic Convention, this time alongside Obama's half-sister, Maya Soetoro-Ng, that 18–18 season three years earlier had the look of a false spring. "Any seven-footers out there, give me a call," he said during their banter onstage. After delivering a shoutout to the First Lady's anti-obesity and nutrition initiatives, he added, "I'm proud of her work to give our children a healthier start in life. And let's face it, Maya: I could use the recruits."

In fact, recruiting hadn't been the problem. Players found their way to Robinson's door, with Roberto Nelson, Devon Collier, and an NBA draft pick, Jared Cunningham, all arriving from high school with impressive credentials. But by the end of the 2013–2014 season Robinson's record stood at 94–105 over six years, with only one winning season. Barely five weeks after delivering a spirited defense of his coach, Oregon State athletic director Bob De Carolis bought out the remaining $4 million of his contract, and Robinson took a gig at his brother-in-law's favorite network, ESPN. ■

On a campaign swing through Chapel Hill in April 2008, the senator challenges 6'9" North Carolina Tar Heel Tyler Hansbrough, the reigning college Player of the Year. (AP Photo/Jae C. Hong.)

RUNNING 3 GAME

In the spring of 2007, several months into his campaign for president, Barack Obama trailed Hillary Clinton by more than thirty points in some polls of Democratic primary voters. That's when Matt Rodriguez, director of Obama's New Hampshire operation, suggested that the candidate play basketball around the Granite State. "If you're a voter in New Hampshire, you might see a candidate seven or eight times," Rodriguez said. "We wanted to carve out something a little different. Plus those are long days, and it's good when the candidate starts them out with a little exercise and something nonpolitical. I don't remember having to twist his arm."

Obama instantly grasped the wisdom of the idea. From his days as a community organizer, he understood that you had to connect with people before you could presume to lead them. Sports can be a powerful way to forge a bond, especially among those who might at first not be inclined to support you. But campaign strategist David Axelrod, who had a record of persuading white voters to back black candidates, wanted to play the hoop card carefully. "People didn't know him well yet, and I didn't want him to play into a stereotype," he said. "Eventually, we loosened the reins."

The first test of Rodriguez's plan came over the summer in Hampton, New Hampshire, where Obama, former Duke captain Reggie Love (see "The Little Brother I Never Had," page 46), and several other aides took on a team of local firefighters. Almost immediately the game turned into a rout. Shortly after Love scored on a layup following a steal, the candidate sidled up to him. "Reggie, we want to win," he said. "But we also want to win their support. . . . Let's just settle down a little bit."

The campaign smartened up. For a game with patrolmen in Manchester, they made sure to mix the teams—although a group of staff and coaches at Southern New Hampshire University, which the Obama crew played as a unit, "was a straight-up team," Rodriguez said. "Even with Reggie on our side, we lost."

To Rodriguez, the hoop vibe around Obama was a striking reversal of what he had experienced two presidential cycles earlier, working on the Bill Bradley campaign. Bradley feared that his background as a former NBA star would keep voters from focusing on his public policy credentials, so even though staffers played regularly, games almost always went off without the candidate taking part. By contrast Obama was as enthusiastic a participant as anyone, which paid

During a May 2008 visit to the Villicana family of Union Mills, Indiana, Obama shoots with Aaron Villicana (*in hat at left*). (AP Photo/Jae C. Hong.)

dividends. "The senator came across as authentic," Rodriguez said. "Like a lot of us, he really liked to play ball."

The Obama campaign also gave basketball a cameo in
Iowa, the other early proving ground in the race for the
nomination. A November 2007 appearance at the Jefferson-Jackson Dinner in Des Moines, where voters tra-
ditionally take the measure of Democratic candidates,
turned into a show of the underdog's strength, as thousands of Obama supporters massed outside the hall and
partisans inside let loose their enthusiasm. In basketball
terms, Hillary Clinton held court, but the upstart had just
swanned through the chain-link fence to call "Next"—and
in case there was any mistaking it, Axelrod brought in Ray
Clay, the Chicago Bulls' P.A. announcer during the Michael
Jordan years, to introduce the candidate. As the Bulls'
pregame introductory music, "Sirius" by the Alan Parsons
Project, swelled in the background, Clay roared, "From our
neighboring state of Illinois, a six-foot-two-inch force for
change, Senator Barack Obama!"

Obama won Iowa emphatically, but five days later he
lost to Clinton in New Hampshire. In February, after placing second again in Super Tuesday nominating contests in

Left: The campaign's Challenge for Change three-on-three tournament
in Kokomo rewarded students who registered the most Indiana voters,
giving them a chance to play with the candidate. During a break in the
action, Obama compares shoe sizes with Tamika Catchings, star of the
WNBA's Indiana Fever. (AP Photo/Jae C. Hong.)

Facing page: In New Castle, Indiana, the senator squeezes off
a shot for the cameras at the Indiana Basketball Hall of Fame.
(AP Photo/Jae C. Hong.)

Ohio and Texas, the campaign looked at a three-month gap before primaries in Indiana and North Carolina. Axelrod decided to change tactics. "We wanted to do campaigning that got us closer to the ground," he said. "More diners and less platform speeches. Basketball was a no-brainer. Besides, any excuse to play is one he'll take."

At the beginning of May, Obama turned up in Chapel Hill to scrimmage with the North Carolina varsity—the generational equivalent, as thirty-five-year-old *Sanford* (N.C.) *Herald* columnist Alex Podlogar put it, of Bill Clinton playing the sax on *Arsenio Hall*. The candidate spent only five minutes on the floor that day and stepped off it breathless. But he sank a jumper, whipped a bounce pass behind his back, and supplied photographers with an image of himself launching a runner in the lane, challenging Tyler Hansbrough, the 6'9" Tar Heel who had just been named college Player of the Year.

• •

Above: Footage of the candidate sinking this three-pointer, during a July 2008 visit to U.S. troops at Camp Arifjan in Kuwait, went viral—and metaphorical. (Department of Defense.)

Facing page: By July 2008, Obama was the presumptive Democratic nominee. Here the senator meets with staff backstage before a rally at a secondary school in Fairfax County, Virginia.
(Photo by Charles Ommanney/Getty Images News/Getty Images.)

In Indiana, both before and after the primary, the campaign struck even more basketball notes. Obama played H-O-R-S-E with a teenager in the town of Union Mills. During a visit to the Indiana Basketball Hall of Fame in New Castle, he sank a "buzzer beater" at an arcade game. And in Kokomo he took part in the campaign's own "Challenge for Change," a three-on-three tournament reserved for youths who had registered the most voters in a statewide competition. The scoreboard in the gym read "HOPE" and "AWAY." On May 6, Obama won North Carolina comfortably and came close in Indiana, essentially locking up the nomination.

Former Tar Heels coach Dean Smith would endorse him before the general election, in which Obama wound up winning North Carolina by a percentage point. He would beat John McCain by the same margin in Indiana, carrying Spencer County, Abraham Lincoln's childhood haunts along the Ohio River, the Euphrates of hoop civilization. Basketball might well have made the difference. A post-election editorial in the Indianapolis *Star* invoked *Hoosiers*, linking Obama's message to one of the film's subplots—how Gene Hackman, playing Hickory High coach Norman Dale, hammers away at hard work, family, and responsibility, even as he extends a hand to the troubled character played by Dennis Hopper: "The community is carefully connected through fundamental values and basketball fundamentals."

Jonathan Singer, a delegate from Longmont, Colorado, wears a knock-off Nuggets jersey to enliven the scene on the floor of the 2008 Democratic National Convention in Denver. (AP Photo/Chris Carlson.)

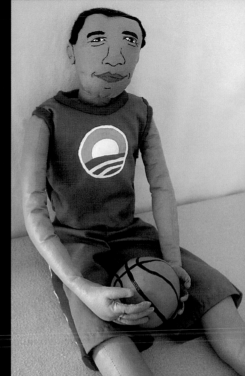

OBAMA
08
GOT NEXT

The historic campaign inspired customized sneakers, hoop-themed tchotchkes, and street art. Ray Noland designed this "Obama Got Next" poster, and Shayna Barry May created a doll—complete with shoes—that she called "Team Captain."
(Poster photo: Ray Noland [formally known as CRO], www.gotellmama.org. Doll and shoes photos: Courtesy of Shayna Barry May.)

Filmmaker and New York Knicks superfan Spike Lee models a T-shirt—inspired by Vince Carter's dunk over Frédéric Weis at the 2000 Sydney Olympics—that depicts Obama posterizing GOP rival John McCain. (Photo by Robyn Beck/AFP/Getty Images.)

With its pivot to the general election over the summer of 2008, the Obama campaign embarked on a tour of eight countries in ten days. The trip was an elaborate exercise in stagecraft, designed to generate still pictures and film footage of someone ready to represent the United States on the world stage. But one of the most enduring images, captured in a gym during a visit to American troops at Camp Arifjan in Kuwait, turned out to be unscripted. In dress pants and street shoes, wearing a microphone and with no warm-up, Obama sent a three-point shot through the net to the cheers of watching soldiers. "He had no business taking a shot with cameras rolling, because the moment screamed metaphor," *Time* would write. But he did, and in the end, said Craig Robinson, "it wasn't that he made or missed that shot. It's that he took it."

The McCain campaign tried desperately to spin the moment as an act of disrespect for the military. The entire international tour, GOP ads and talking points charged, was an indulgence by an empty celebrity who craved the spotlight. But over the rest of the campaign that film footage cut another way—as symbolic evidence of Obama as the man with the magic touch. More literally, recalled Julius Genachowski, the old Harvard Law pickup buddy who worked on the campaign, "the video alerted a broader audience that the guy could shoot. Basketball started to get more attention."

The game had been his lifelong companion, and now, in the political fight of Obama's life, it was pulling its weight. Basketball metaphors, never far from the candidate's lips, began to crop up among aides too. "There had been the tumultuous run-up to the first debate where we weren't sure

McCain would show up," Axelrod said. "We're standing in the green room and he's about to take the stage, and I could have easily gone to the bathroom and thrown up. So I ask him how he's feeling. 'I'm a little nervous, but it's a good nervous,' he says. 'Give me the ball. Let's play the game.' He has that mentality great athletes have. He wants to take the shot."

But the campaign wasn't peddling an unbridled playground persona. Two weeks before Election Day, Obama sounded much like his old Punahou coach, or members of his pedigreed basketball crew back in Chicago. With the economy teetering and the electorate looking for a sober head, slow and steady was the order of the day. "Every time we've gotten in trouble in this campaign," Obama said on NBC's *Today*, "it's because we stopped trying to play ball-control offense."

On a deeper level, basketball undermined Republican efforts to portray Obama as foreign, suspicious, or someone who "pals around with terrorists." When playing pickup, he was palling around with pals, engaging in the most democratic iteration of a game that touched people on the streets of Compton, to be sure, but also in the ward halls of Provo and the manicured parks north of Indianapolis. The game laid out a powerful counternarrative, according to Duke anthropologist Orin Starn, an effective way of saying, "'See, I'm not a crazy Muslim. . . . I'm one of the guys; I know how to do the guy culture.'"

Or as Sen. Robert Casey, who played with Obama on the campaign trail in his home state of Pennsylvania, put it: "It's such an American thing to do. And it's the way he communicates."

As the game around which the Obama campaign organized itself, basketball eventually took on a talismanic

meaning. On the morning of the Iowa caucuses, unable to campaign because of anti-electioneering rules, Obama and several aides found a gym, roped the building supervisor into the game to make a quorum, and played. Obama would eventually do so again, with aides and friends and Secret Service agents, on the day of every caucus or primary he won (Iowa, North Carolina, South Carolina), and fail to play on the day of those he lost (New Hampshire and Nevada). On Super Tuesday, when he won more states and picked up more delegates than Clinton, he played at the closest thing to a home court, Chicago's East Bank Club.

On November 4, with the ultimate balloting in the balance, no one on the campaign was prepared to abandon a superstition that worked. Some thirty-five aides, associates, and friends, including three from his Punahou days, converged on Chicago's Attack Athletics complex to play a four-team, round-robin tournament while the votes were counted. Friends Marty Nesbitt and Eric Whitaker helped Obama choose the teams. Illinois state treasurer Alexi Giannoulias, playing off a dismissive remark McCain had made about Obama in one of the debates, brought reversible jerseys so the teams could be divided into "This One" and "That One."

Late that afternoon, exit poll data began pinballing among Obama's aides. Early returns would soon be trickling in from nearby Indiana and Kentucky. The candidate could have been riding his BlackBerry between games, trying to catch a glimpse of his future. Instead, true to the end, "he go play hoop."

"You nervous?" one player asked Obama during a break.

"There's nothing I can do," the president-in-waiting replied. "Everything's done."

"The Little Brother I Never Had"

In a 1999 episode from the first season of *The West Wing,* when President Josiah Bartlet plays a fierce game of half-court pickup with aides, he makes sure his team includes one Rodney Grant, associate director of the President's Council on Physical Fitness and a former player at Duke. The ringer, played on the show by then-NBA star Juwan Howard, sends a critical Toby Ziegler shot into the bushes off the South Lawn to assure President Bartlet's team of victory.

In the annals of life imitating art, there are few better examples than what happened over the decade after that episode aired. In 2006 Sen. Barack Obama (D-Ill.) added to his staff an assistant named Reggie Love, who had played on Duke's 2001 NCAA title team. Though recruited for football, Love adored basketball and somehow made the team as a walk-on. His coach, Mike Krzyzewski, went volcanic after photos of Love, passed out on a futon at a party on the North Carolina campus surrounded by fraternity brothers straddling his face, went viral.

Several months later Love was stopped at the wheel of his car and booked for underage drinking. But he went on to become the first walk-on in school history to be both a starter and captain. A political science and public policy major, he spent the summer after his sophomore year in Indiana, working for Bloomington mayor John Fernandez's campaign for secretary of state. "There's no task too small for him," Krzyzewski told Obama's people when they called. That, Obama chief of staff Pete Rouse would later say, was why the senator hired Love, who eventually ascended to "chief of stuff."

Love's first duties were in the mailroom, logging letters, most in response to Obama's well-received keynote address at the 2004 Democratic National Convention. He lived in a crash pad in Northeast D.C., supplementing his Senate wages as a bouncer at an Irish pub. Within a year he was promoted to the role of personal aide, or "body man," which meant providing dawn-to-wee-hours support and never being without breath mints, Nicorette gum, and a Tide stain-remover pen. Obama came to call Love both his "iReggie," font of

all things tech and pop cultural ("so that I'm not a complete fuddy duddy"), and "the little brother I never had."

Their exchanges inevitably turned to hoop. Basketball, Love has written, "modified the tenor of our interactions and took us from boss and underling to something more like friends." During the 2007 NBA Playoffs they debated the merits of Chris Paul versus Tony Parker, sending each other can-you-top-this stat lines by late-night e-mail. (Love stood up for his Tar Heel State compatriot; Obama made the case for the San Antonio Spur with the biracial background.) After Obama decided to pursue the presidency, they smoothed over the rough edges of the road with early morning runs, beginning in New Hampshire. Obama quickly laid down a rule: "No one takes it easy on me."

After Obama won the White House, Love jawboned pilots into radioing ahead for NCAA tournament updates or the latest score of the Bulls game, and logged gifts left by championship teams after White House visits (see "The World's Most Elegant Locker Room," page 97). All the while he tried to keep up with an executive M.B.A. program at Penn's

Wharton School, but juggling so many obligations left him on the verge of flunking out. Three years into the president's first term, after traveling millions of miles and visiting every state and sixty-five countries, he left the White House to attend Wharton full-time.

Upon graduation in 2013 Love joined Transatlantic Holdings, a private equity firm, as a partner. He taught an evening class at Georgetown and joined a couple of start-ups with digital twists—a mobile app for ordering concessions at sporting events and software to help parents monitor their kids' use of social media. He also served as an advisor to the successful 2015 reelection campaign of British prime minister David Cameron before joining VICE Sports as editor-at-large. "The problem is, I won't hire an assistant," said Love, sounding like someone for whom no task truly is too small. "Even though it makes no sense not to have one, I'm going to be a better assistant than anyone I hire."

Life did depart slightly from *The West Wing* once Obama settled into the White House. "On the campaign

we used to play on the same team all the time," Love said, neglecting to mention how much this irritated those marooned on the other side, who invariably lost. "After he got to the White House, we started to mix it up, old guys vs. young. I'd usually play with the young. And the old guys kicked our butts."∎

Reggie Love's service to Barack Obama began in 2006, in the mailroom of the Illinois senator's office. By the time he left the White House in 2011, after countless games of pickup and H-O-R-S-E, the former Duke captain had traveled with the president to every state in the union and sixty-five countries. (Pete Souza/The White House.)

Running Game

DO NOT
DUNK BALLS
or HANG on RIM!

Obama, One-on-One

Character studies of Barack Obama the ballplayer typically assess him as a teammate in a game of full-court five-on-five. It's the configuration that invites answers to the essential question: Does he play well with others? But one-on-one scrambles the circumstances, offering a different light by which to judge him. And the best-documented instance of Obama playing one-on-one took place in December 2007, at a YMCA in Spencer, Iowa, not quite two weeks before he won that state's caucuses and assumed so much political velocity that he wouldn't play basketball with a solo opponent for public consumption again.

Early that morning *Sports Illustrated* senior writer S. L. (Scott) Price played the candidate twice,

. . . .

Facing page: To evoke their shared love of Dr. J, *Sports Illustrated* writer Scott Price brought ABA colors to his December 2007 match-up with Senator Obama at the Spencer, Iowa, YMCA. Obama wore businesslike black and threw competitive shade on the court, beating Price in both games. (Photo by Bill Frakes/*Sports Illustrated*/Getty Images.)

while photographer Bill Frakes shot still pictures and Price's son, Jack, then eleven, let a video camera run.

"He showed his teeth a little bit with my son beforehand, pumping him for information about my game," Price recalled. Jack gave his dad up: weak jump shot; not in "basketball shape."

At the latter, Obama nodded. "There's a difference," he told Jack. "All the stopping and starting."

Then the candidate turned to Jack's dad. "All right," he said. "I got your game cased out."

And so they began, playing "make it, take it" with the ABA ball Price had brought along. Its red, white, and blue pattern both resembled Obama's campaign logo and evoked the vintage Julius Erving poster that Obama and Price had each hung over his bed as a kid.

Sometimes Obama would yell "*Woooo!*" when Price let fly an outside shot, gamesmanship that Price remembered as "a little bit cheap." But the senator compensated for that, Price recalled: "He didn't call ticky-tack fouls if they didn't affect his shot."

One time Price bodied the candidate as Obama flipped up an underhand shot in the lane. "You want to call it?" Price asked. "I got you seven different ways there."

Obama waved him off. "He knew it wasn't that honorable a shot," Price would say later. "Even though [a foul call] was justified, the shot was lame, so he didn't call one."

Obama beat Price 11–5 in that game. They then sat for an interview, in which Obama wondered why Price, with advantages of fifteen pounds and at least an inch, hadn't backed him down more.

Price did exactly that when the two resumed play, and he fared better for it. When Obama found a clear path to the basket after getting the benefit of an oddly caroming rebound, Price hard-fouled the candidate rather than surrender a chippy. The moment led Price to think briefly back to something Michelle Obama had told him a few days earlier: "Don't break his nose, give him a black eye or knock his teeth out. Or I'll have to come find you."

"Believe me," Obama said, accepting the benefit of that foul with a nod at the Secret Service agents in the gym. "You can get shot for that."

Late in that second game Obama handed the ball to Price for a check. Price flipped it back to him near the top of key and said, "O.K. This is for the presidency."

Obama squeezed off a jumper from just inside the arc that swished cleanly through.

Price: "You heard what I said, right?"
Obama: "Why do you think I hit it?"

The candidate had to be somewhere, so the two agreed to put five minutes on the clock. "The question is whether we can [finish] without a defibrillator," Obama said.

Later Price would say, "He has no right hand, but I was so gassed I couldn't take advantage of it." At full time of Game Two, Obama stood up 7–5.

In his notebook afterward, Price made these observations: "Absolutely comfortable in his own skin . . . not looking to impress . . . none of the underlying anxiety or ambition [of] Washington types you can sense are always measuring each word and act as pieces in an endless competition of one-upmanship."

"I came away from the whole thing thinking he didn't need us," Price would say years later. "He has that Kennedy cool. He wasn't like Clinton, growing up thinking he's got to be president. That was part of his appeal, that he wasn't like Clinton or Nixon."

From a couple of games of one-on-one, Price caught a glimpse of a man at ease with the give-and-take of pickup ball, possessed of a thorough understanding of one-on-one's unwritten code, and brimming with confidence. "After that, he was pretty much a runaway train," Price remembered. "But nothing I learned about him later in the campaign really surprised me."■

Players' Choice

Among many examples of the reputed indifference of pro basketball players to the world around them, few are more memorable than the comment of Orlando Magic center Shaquille O'Neal after he returned from a trip to Greece in 1994. Asked whether he had visited the Parthenon, O'Neal replied, "Man, I can't remember the names of all the clubs we went to." Whether Shaq was genuinely oblivious or the Big Aristotle was playing dumb, an almost proud insularity could be found around the league—or it could be until Barack Obama's campaign began to stir NBA players from their torpor.

A procession of presidents had wanted to catch the reflected glory of prominent sports stars, but here things began to work in the opposite direction. Journeyman guard Baron Davis first met Obama in Washington in 2006, when Davis dropped by the freshman senator's office to pitch him on his youth development foundation. When Obama announced his run for president, Davis swung into action,

hosting fundraisers, passing out campaign literature in locker rooms, and pulling the levers of social media.

As the campaign advanced, other players fell in line. Kevin Garnett of the Boston Celtics scrawled, "Vote for Change" on his shoes. LeBron James of the Cleveland Cavaliers joined hip-hop artist Jay-Z to lead a get-out-the-vote rally in Ohio, while Chauncey Billups, then with the Detroit Pistons, introduced the candidate at an event in Michigan. Though he would come up sixteen points short, the Denver Nuggets' Carmelo Anthony pledged before a game to score forty-four points for the prospective forty-fourth president. The Washington Wizards' Gilbert Arenas, who had once called himself "Black President," indicated that he was ready to peacefully relinquish the title when he tattooed four words—"Change We Believe In"—on his left hand, one on each finger. On Election Day in 2008, the Houston Rockets' Steve Francis showed up for a home game wearing a red velvet sports jacket with the candidate's name spelled out in sequins on the back.

Obama's candidacy captivated

even non-American NBA players. The Dallas Mavericks' Dirk Nowitzki wasn't among the 200,000 Germans who packed Berlin's Tiergarten in July 2008 to hear Obama speak, but Nowitzki, back in his homeland at the time, had watched on TV, mesmerized. "He talked about how the world is global and we're all coming together," he said. "He was already being celebrated like he was the President."

Despite finding themselves in the middle of their season, some NBA teams canceled practice to allow players to watch the 2009 inauguration live on TV, and the Boston Celtics' Ray Allen and the Houston Rockets' Dikembe Mutombo arranged to attend. For Mutombo, a native of the Congo who became a U.S. citizen in 2006, the chance to vote in his first presidential election had particular resonance, he said, because the Kenyan American "has the same roots and the same blood with me."

The possibility of an African American reaching the White House surely helped energize the league's overwhelmingly black labor pool. But the dawning political consciousness in

NBA locker rooms had a generational component too. Millennials were more willing to wave the banner of idealism than their Generation X or Baby Boomer counterparts. Meanwhile smartphones and social media gave players a quick, personal way to connect with one another and fans alike. For his part, Allen actually credited the players' extravagant wealth with leading so many to get involved. "You can do more with your money," he said. "You can be more philanthropic, and most guys have foundations. I always tell guys, whether they like it or not, we're all political at some point."

Thus when friends and aides planned a round-robin basketball tournament to celebrate Obama's forty-ninth birthday in August 2010, they had little trouble inducing two dozen current and former NBA players to come to Washington to help populate four teams. The guest list included such stars as James and Chris Paul, members of Obama's hometown Chicago Bulls such as Derrick Rose and Joakim Noah, and retired greats Magic Johnson and Bill Russell.

The bond remained when Obama came up for reelection two years later. Johnson, Vince Carter, and Alonzo Mourning hosted fundraisers. And in August 2012 several dozen active and former NBA and WNBA stars, including Anthony, Patrick Ewing, Penny Hardaway, Michael Jordan, Paul Pierce, Sheryl Swoopes, and Dawn Staley, turned up in Manhattan for what the campaign billed as the Obama Classic, a $20,000-a-plate fundraiser with photo ops and a shootaround folded in.

In 2008 and again in 2012, the average NBA salary of more than $5 million put virtually everyone in the league in the crosshairs of Obama's proposals to raise taxes on high-end earners. Yet players largely sloughed off any concern. The reaction of Utah Jazz forward Carlos Boozer was typical. "My mom and dad ain't making what I'm making," he said. "My brothers and sisters ain't making what I'm making. My cousins ain't making what I'm making. My friends ain't. But if they get better, then I'm happy. 'Cause our country gets better." ∎

. . . .

Facing page: The president checks in with hometown heroes Joakim Noah (*left*) and Derrick Rose of the Chicago Bulls during his birthday game at D.C.'s Fort McNair in August 2011. The blue reversible jerseys read "POTUS 49th." (Pete Souza/The White House.)

The president and the First Lady watch the retiring of the colors before North Carolina and Michigan State tip off in the 2011 Carrier Classic, staged on the flight deck of the USS *Carl Vinson* in San Diego Bay. (Pete Souza/The White House.)

POWER, 4 FORWARD

Just as Barack Obama made a conscious decision to raise himself as "a black man in America," he chose as a young adult male to continue to cast his lot with basketball. And his comfort with that latter identity didn't evaporate when he arrived in the White House. If anything, the game led him and his baller's profile to stand out even more starkly against the broad, golf-inflected monochrome of official Washington. An African American president was an astonishment, as unlikely as a five-foot point guard who could dunk, wrote the black critic Ta-Nehisi Coates. "And yet," Coates added, referring to a 5'7" NBA Slam Dunk Champion from the eighties, "Spud Webb lives."

Race nonetheless had a way of seeming to tie Obama's hands. As a candidate he had made pains to pledge to serve as president of all the people, and after wading into controversy early in his first term over an altercation between a black Harvard professor and a white Cambridge policeman, he seemed reluctant to take the issue up. Through his first two years in office Obama mentioned race and racial issues in proclamations, news conferences, and executive orders less often than any Democratic president since the sixties. In the aftermath of the killing of an unarmed teenager in Florida in 2012, he would declare, "If I had a son, he'd look like Trayvon Martin"—a poignant sentiment, but one that was also self-evident.

Things changed perceptibly after his reelection in 2012. Obama arranged for the transition of My Brother's Keeper, a White House initiative for young minority men, to the My Brother's Keeper Alliance, a nonprofit that figured to be a focus of his efforts after leaving office. He spoke movingly

and forcefully after the Charleston church shootings. And en route to ceremonies marking the fiftieth anniversary of the Selma march, he underscored for a half-dozen black journalists on Air Force One his commitment to issues of concern to African Americans, even if "I don't always say it the way I might say it if I'm on the basketball court with some of my buddies." He also reminded them that, in the wake of the deaths at the hands of the police of such unarmed black men as Michael Brown and Eric Garner, comments he made couldn't be seen as "putting thumbs on the scale" and jeopardizing the course of the legal system.

His remarks about race nonetheless had a way of sounding more muted than the moment called for. When Obama performed a routine at the 2015 White House Correspondents' Dinner with Luther the Anger Translator, played by African American comedian Keegan-Michael Key, he signaled at least some self-awareness of his reputation for pulling punches. "He has been very measured on race," said Dave Zirin, sports editor of *The Nation*. "Yet basketball, he's let run."

Perhaps he continued to embrace the game because, in an America driven more and more by the tastes of a growing nonwhite and Millennial population, basketball and urban cultural adjacencies like music and fashion had spilled beyond the bounds of race. The sport found followers in almost every segment of Obama's political coalition.

. . . .

Taking a break from inspecting the effects of drought on farms in the Midwest, Obama plays ball in the driveway of the McIntosh family in Harrison County, Iowa, in August 2012. (Pete Souza/The White House.)

As an October 2014 meeting with participants in the White House mentoring program wound down, one mentee challenged the president to a game of H-O-R-S-E. "Let's go," replied Obama, who led the group from the Roosevelt Room to the South Lawn court. Here the former community organizer continues to engage the group in life lessons. (Pete Souza/The White House.)

Passion for the game reached even into largely white, red-state markets like Salt Lake, Oklahoma City, and Kentucky. Most NBA players may have been African American, but those who weren't now included natives of dozens of different countries. And Jeremy Lin, who in 2012 landed on the covers of both *Time* and *Sports Illustrated,* proved that even an Asian American pro basketball player could take a star turn.

Or maybe Obama's being true to hoop represented that rarest of things: a politician content to let the public see exactly who he was. On the eve of his inauguration in 1905, Teddy Roosevelt sparred with a professional prizefighter; on the eve of his, the forty-fourth president-to-be, who had the NBA's League Pass app loaded on his iPad, shot hoops in a D.C. gym.

The basketball idiom so prevalent during the campaign also found a home in the White House. A few weeks after assuming office, Obama described Vice President Joe Biden as someone "who does a bunch of things that don't show up in the stat sheet. He gets that extra rebound, takes the charge, makes that extra pass." In a fundraising letter to supporters, calling for innovation to respond to global challenges, he declared, "We need to up our game." "We're the Miami Heat and he's Jeremy Lin," he told Democratic governors at a February 2012 retreat, in a refer-

ence to likely GOP opponent Mitt Romney, shortly after the Heat had throttled the New York Knicks' rookie star in a widely anticipated game. During the quailing days of the 2012 campaign, the president described the state of play in familiar terms: Tight game, fourth quarter, Team Obama "up a few points" against a Romney campaign "coming on strong" and playing "a little dirty."

The argot with which Obama felt so comfortable could lay the occasional snare. In a January 2014 interview with the *New Yorker,* speaking of upstart Islamist terrorist groups like ISIS, he said, "If a jayvee team puts on Lakers uniforms, that doesn't make them Kobe Bryant." The interviewer, David Remnick, called it "an uncharacteristically flip analogy," and by August, events in Iraq and Syria would lead Obama to commit U.S. assets to fight the very kind of Al Qaeda–inspired organization he seemed to dismiss.

And Reggie Love's old college coach, Mike Krzyzewski, proved that two could play the hoopspeak game. In remarks to the Association of the United States Army in November 2014, Krzyzewski didn't mention the president or the Islamic State by name. But the incumbent U.S. men's national team coach took an indirect shot at Obama's position on ISIS while stretching basketball analogy to the breaking point. A stated policy not to send ground troops, Krzyzewski said, was like handing your playbook to an opponent. "I'm not [going to say], 'Hey, Spain, I'm not going to start LeBron and Kobe tonight.' . . . The fact that we're a free country, and we don't play home games here, is a result of having boots on the ground."

At times Washington seemed at risk of getting sucked into a vortex of basketball lingo, where rhetoric over-

Power,

Forward

Facing page: The president played often and vigorously during his first several years in office. Here, with aides and their family members around him, he goes up strong with his left hand during a July 2009 run at Camp David. (Pete Souza/The White House.)

whelmed the substance it sought to illuminate. But with its metaphorical ubiquity, basketball had a way of crossing party lines. When freshman congressman and former Purdue captain Curt Clawson of Florida delivered the Tea Party response to Obama's 2015 State of the Union address, he drew on the game to sketch out both an opposing political vision and the country's acute political division. "At Purdue, our biggest challenge was never the other team," Clawson said. "It was in our own locker room."

How does a presidency use a sport to govern? Obama showed how with small, symbolic gestures and larger tactical plays alike. On Father's Day in 2009, Dwyane Wade of the Miami Heat and Etan Thomas of the Washington Wizards joined Hall of Famer Alonzo Mourning at the White House for the launch of the president's fatherhood initiative, where they heard Obama say that one of the sacrifices he makes as a dad is that he couldn't "watch D-Wade on *SportsCenter*" as often as he'd like. At an event tied to her Let's Move anti-obesity initiative, Michelle Obama dunked a mini-basketball on LeBron James while Wade ticked off tips for healthy eating. Mourning eventually joined Grant Hill, Chris Paul, and Jason Collins on what was once called the President's Council on Physical Fitness but under Obama became the President's Council on Fitness, Sports and Nutrition to better reflect the priorities of the president and the First Lady. Those four basketball players overwhelmed the representation on the council of every other sport.

The game played its biggest role during the implementation of health-care reform in 2013 and 2014. After the balky rollout of HealthCare.gov, political analysts began to prepare obituaries for the Affordable Care Act. Obamacare appeared unlikely to entice enough young, healthy enrollees to broaden the risk pool and help underwrite the older, more costly people who would need less persuasion to sign up. That's when basketball came to the rescue. The NBA season coincided almost exactly with the law's six-month open-enrollment period, from October through March. And the league's fans tended to be young and to include groups, especially blacks, Latinos, and single men, with large numbers of uninsured. To reach them the Department of Health and Human Services booked ad space on ESPN, TNT, ABC, and NBAtv, as well as local stations in markets with high concentrations of targeted populations.

When they learned of the administration's plan, political opponents howled in protest. GOP senators Mitch McConnell of Kentucky and John Cornyn of Texas wrote all the major sports leagues, urging them to report any instance in which they felt they were being targeted with some "policy consequence" for failing to cooperate with a White House trying to sell Obamacare. "I would caution you against being coerced into doing their dirty work for them," wrote Rep. Steve Scalise (R-La.) to NBA commissioner David Stern and NFL commissioner Roger Goodell. Yet the Obama administration was pursuing the same

. . . .

Facing page: The president greets Wounded Warriors from Walter Reed National Military Medical Center when they play a game on the White House court in July 2011. (Pete Souza/The White House.)

strategy as Massachusetts in 2007, when that state partnered with the Boston Red Sox to educate citizens about its new health-care regime, signed into law by the state's governor, one Mitt Romney.

Once the HealthCare.gov website began to function, the White House pressed its campaign on multiple fronts. First came thirty-second TV spots from two former players, each the survivor of a sudden medical calamity in the prime of his career. In a spot that also aired during college basketball games, Magic Johnson didn't have to allude specifically to HIV, for he had long been the public face of the AIDS virus. Affordable coverage, he said in that public service announcement, "might sound like Magic. But take my word for it. It's real."

For his TV spot, Alonzo Mourning recounted how he had been struck down by a kidney ailment. "I was at the top of my game. I felt invincible. But when I went for my regular team physical, it turned out I had a serious kidney disease."

After a transplant, Mourning was able to return to action and help the Heat win an NBA title, which lent even more power to his outcue: "Enroll today so you can stay in the game."

Then, for the final push to the sign-up deadline of March 31, 2014, the administration played off March Madness. The White House posted Obama's NCAA tournament

Alonzo Mourning (*center*) and Grant Hill both served on the President's Council on Fitness, Sports and Nutrition. Mourning played an influential role during Obama's presidency as both Affordable Care Act spokesperson and golfing buddy. (Pete Souza/The White House.)

bracket on the ACA website, where visitors could vote in a video contest on the theme of "The 16 Sweetest Reasons to Get Covered." (The winner, "Women Can't Be Charged More Than Men," featured Michelle Obama and LeBron James jointly videobombing Miami Heat teammates Wade and Ray Allen, as well as coach Erik Spoelstra.) HHS blasted out data: Nearly 600,000 people had visited emergency rooms for basketball-related injuries during 2012, with a sprain typically costing more than $2,200 to treat. To underscore the implications of those numbers, another member of the Heat, former Duke star Shane Battier, recited the medical toll since he began to play competitively a quarter century earlier: more than ninety stitches, at least twenty-five ankle sprains, broken elbows, a reconstructed ankle, and arthritis in his knees and hip.

Finally, the White House enlisted three more active stars to film solo PSAs—James, Wade, and Kobe Bryant. All had visited the Obama White House as NBA champions, and each used social media channels to amplify his appeal to sign up for coverage. Consider the value the administration derived from the campaign: James collected more than $40 million annually in endorsement income; Obamacare got its LeBron testimonial for free.

Nor was Obama above mining his own recreational basketball career for cautionary tales. In December 2013, shortly after HealthCare.gov had begun to function relatively smoothly, he alluded to that injury back in law school. "In my 20s and early 30s I thought I was invincible, but it turns out I broke my nose playing basketball," he told Fusion, a network targeting Millennial audiences. "There were times where I had unexpected illnesses or acci-

dents, and making sure that you've got coverage ensures that you're not ending up paying out of pocket thousands of dollars that you may not have."

As the first deadline for ACA sign-ups in year two approached, he reprised that message in a similarly personal way. "For all you weekend warriors, by the time I got to about 40, basketball was pretty hazardous," he told ESPN Radio host Colin Cowherd, who began the interview by shouting out an 800 number and the HealthCare.gov web address. "You don't want to . . . suddenly have something broken or something pop—because it's gonna cost you a lot of money. Eighty-two bucks a month is the average premium when you take into account the tax credits. I hope everybody signs up. It's the smart thing to do."

Despite the debacle of the HealthCare.gov rollout, the ACA confounded skeptics and met its enrollment targets. Obama's ability to call in favors from basketball greats likely played a critical role. "I appreciate that LeBron and Magic and other folks helped drive this message about getting health insurance," he said. "When you think about some of our greatest sports heroes, Muhammad Ali, Bill Russell, Arthur Ashe, they spoke out on issues that mattered at pretty critical times."

No American sport has been exported more widely than basketball, and the Obama administration took unprecedented advantage of the game's international influence. Bill Clinton had been passionate about college basketball, appearing on the cover of *Sports Illustrated* in Arkansas regalia on the eve of the 1994 NCAA tournament that his Razorbacks won, but the appeal of the college game stopped at the water's edge. Obama's basketball invocations usually featured the NBA, which projected globally in a way that Clinton's Hogs could not. In 2012, when Obama took British prime minister David Cameron to a first-round NCAA tournament game in Dayton, he was sharing with his visitor a cultural idiosyncrasy, the American equivalent of Cameron taking Obama to Lord's Cricket Ground for a test match. An NBA star, by contrast, operated on the same international celebrity plane as a head of state.

To help repair relations with Spanish prime minister José Luis Rodríguez Zapatero, who had angered the Bush administration by withdrawing Spanish troops from Iraq, Obama bonded over their shared birthday (August 4, one year apart), two daughters, and common love of basketball. And when the president made an appearance overseas, he would drop any relevant basketball reference. A week after the Dallas Mavericks won the 2011 NBA title, Obama namechecked guard J. J. Barea, saying, "That guy can play!" during the first presidential visit to Puerto Rico in fifty years. He shouted out Senegalese draft prospect Gorgui Dieng during a toast at a state dinner in Dakar. In a speech to the Turkish parliament he declared that NBA players Hedo Turkoglu and Mehmet Okur had "game." Knowing that Tanzanian president Jakaya Kikwete played ball in high school and loved LeBron James, Obama came through Dar es Salaam bearing gifts of a LeBron jersey and shoes. (In light of George W. Bush's having already given Kikwete size 23 Shaquille O'Neal sneakers, a closet in the presidential palace, at One Barack Obama Drive, was filling up quite nicely.) "Basketball is having so much growth globally," said Reggie Love, the president's personal aide, "that it's a huge icebreaker."

Hoop gestures went in the other direction too. Several years before facilitating Obama's dramatic opening with Cuba, Canadian prime minister Stephen Harper gave the president a basketball, signed by the 2010–2011 Toronto Raptors, in a leather-bound box graced with the seal of Harper's office. During the July 2009 G-8 summit in L'Aquila, in central Italy, prime minister Silvio Berlusconi arranged for a half-court to be built in a police compound for Obama's enjoyment. In March 2014, as an official gift, the Belgian government gave the president a nearly life-sized *speculaas* cookie baked in the likeness of Obama dribbling a basketball.

When Obama was enjoying a state dinner with German chancellor Angela Merkel in Berlin, you could find Dallas Mavericks star Dirk Nowitzki at the table; when the president attended a similar gala with Australian prime minister Julia Gillard in Canberra, there was NBA guard Patty Mills, who had grown up a few miles away, in the receiving line. On an April morning in 2009, only hours after Obama's pick in his NCAA tournament bracket won the national championship, the president met in Turkey with the Archbishop of Istanbul. "Oh, and by the way," the Ecumenical Patriarch said during their meeting, "congratulations on North Carolina."

The administration also deployed basketball far from the pomp of high-level diplomacy. From the time she took office, Secretary of State Hillary Clinton pressed an approach to international relations that she called "smart power," which involved deploying cultural assets to project American interests and values. Two initiatives run by the

State Department's Bureau of Educational and Cultural Affairs became more focused on basketball during Clinton's term of service. The programs, gathered under the umbrella of SportsUnited, worked in tandem: Sports Envoys sent American athletes and coaches overseas to teach a sport and preach its associated lessons; Sports Visitors brought foreign athletes, usually teens selected by U.S. embassies, to the States for two weeks of playing games, attending clinics, and learning about healthy living, diversity, and conflict resolution. For three years after SportsUnited's founding in 2005, the Bush administration sent abroad nineteen sports envoys with basketball backgrounds. In Obama's first six years, the State Department dispatched seventy-nine, and by 2014 basketball represented some 70 percent of all the participants in the program, more than twice the percentage of hoop envoys under Bush.

It helped that, beginning in 2011, the NBA supplied SportsUnited with in-kind support and that the assistant secretary of state who in 2013 took charge of educational and cultural affairs, Evan Ryan, was the daughter of two major-college ballplayers and the sister of another. "I like to think the basketball focus was partially inspired by the President," Ryan said. "It can be a powerful tool for bridging divides, especially in places where people may not be as receptive to American assistance or help. You're showing

Dirk Nowitzki of the Dallas Mavericks chats with Obama and German chancellor Angela Merkel in Berlin's Charlottenburg Palace during a 2013 state visit. With the president's basketball passion well known to his overseas hosts, diplomatic events frequently went off with a hoop twist. (Pete Souza/The White House.)

them something that's quintessentially American, expos-
ing them to American culture, but in a lot of places it's also
relatively new."

That can be critical in trying to engage teams of Arabs
and Jews in Israel, or Protestants and Catholics in Belfast.
"No one has too much of an advantage," said Ryan. "It gives
them a chance to learn something together."

Places touched by SportsUnited basketball exchanges
during the Obama era included both postconflict countries, such as Angola, Lebanon, and the Congo, and hot
spots where preemptive peacebuilding made sense, such
as Ukraine, Georgia, and Jerusalem. The State Department
liked basketball's suitability to both genders and actually
sent abroad more WNBA than NBA players. "It's a policy

. . . .

decision," Ryan said of the emphasis on women, which her department served with its Empowering Girls and Women through Sports initiative and Global Sports Mentoring Program. "If you can empower one woman to go back and give back in her own community, there's a multiplier effect. You can challenge stereotypes, lift girls up, and completely change the trajectory of their lives."

One of SportsUnited's most successful examples of bilateral basketball involved Burma, a former pariah state that, after Obama's election, began a transition from military dictatorship to democracy. In August 2012 Charlotte Bobcats general manager Rich Cho, a Burmese immigrant, joined a Sports Envoys delegation that included former NBA players Darvin Ham and Marty Conlon and former WNBA player Allison Feaster. Three months later Obama became the first sitting U.S. president to visit Burma, pledging economic aid and the appointment of the first U.S. ambassador to Rangoon since 1990.

Then, in January 2013, the Sports Visitors program brought a dozen athletically and academically promising Burmese teenagers, six boys and six girls, to the United States. They jumped into pregame warm-ups at a Wizards game and took on a coed team of varsity players at Maryland's Walter Johnson High School. In Charlotte they worked out with local teams and visited a Bobcats game

as Cho's guests. None of the young Burmese could miss the power of the Charlotte GM's story: Cho's father had served as editor of a newspaper critical of the military regime, which forced the family to flee to the United States in 1968, when Cho was three. Growing up outside Seattle, Cho trained as an engineer and a lawyer before becoming the NBA's first Asian American GM, with the Portland Trail Blazers in 2010.

Burmese basketball wasn't well established. But the sport had become widely popular among youth elsewhere in Asia and figured to grow in Burma as that country opened up. Meanwhile the U.S. relationship with China, troubled by recurrent differences over cyberattacks and trade, could always return to the safe ground of hoop. China counted millions more NBA fans than did the country over which Obama presided, and midway through the president's second term the league staged, in Beijing and Shanghai, preseason games between the Sacramento Kings and the Brooklyn Nets. In greeting a Chinese delegation in Washington for strategic and economic talks in 2009, Obama presented Vice-Premier Wang Qishan with a basketball and invoked that country's most famous migrant worker. "I have learned from the words of Yao Ming," he said. "No matter whether you are a new or an old team member, you need time to adjust to one another."

These were apt comments when a new president, Xi Jinping, took power in Beijing four years later. As the world's two biggest emitters of carbon announced a climate deal in late 2014, Obama stood in the Great Hall of the People alongside Xi, who before and after his ascent to China's presidency had dropped in on Lakers games.

During a break in the 2009 G-8 Summit in the remote Italian town of L'Aquila, Obama and his aides take advantage of a makeshift court built for his enjoyment in a police compound on the orders of his host, Prime Minister Silvio Berlusconi. (Pete Souza/The White House.)

Facing page: British prime minister David Cameron joins Obama courtside for an NCAA men's tournament First Four game between Western Kentucky and Mississippi Valley State in Dayton in 2012. (Pete Souza/The White House.)

Obama would come in for criticism for a kind of ad hoc foreign policy. But if the president's approach to international relations had a pickup quality—if his backcourt playing style (run the offense, avoid turnovers, get the ball in the right hands at the right time) could be described, like America's role in the world after the Iraq War, as "leading from behind"—Obama had internalized that posture over a basketball lifetime of temporary alliances and tactical adaptations. In pickup ball, said Claude Johnson of Baller-in-Chief.com, "since you never know whose side you're going to be on the next time around, you're not interested in destroying teammates." You choose teams, then form and re-form them, doing your best with whatever hand you're dealt to hold court and play another game.

The White House basketball court was essentially the South Lawn tennis court with stanchions plunked down at either end. This space, fringed by dogwoods and pines, alternated between a presidential stage set and Obama's personal playground. One day in May 2010, while it was being used as the former, the president offered a glimpse into its value as the latter. "I probably play once every two or three weeks, not as often as I'd like," he told TNT's Marv Albert during a sit-down interview on the court. "But during, say, the health-care debate, when things are just going crazy over on Capitol Hill, a lot of times I'll just come out here and shoot or I'll play a game of H-O-R-S-E. It takes an edge off things."

The remark indicated how the game played a therapeutic role. "There's no question to me that basketball was his outlet," said Arthur Jackson, who worked with Reggie Love to recruit players for the president's full-court games. "He could go on the court and escape from everything."

Early in his presidency, in the middle of a work day, Obama and Love would frequently make that short walk to the court, where the president shed his suitcoat and spent twenty minutes or so trying to pin the letters of H-O-R-S-E on his personal aide. "Those of us around him all the time came to see that he very seldom sweats," said Pete Souza, the official White House photographer, who would document those sessions. "It annoyed the hell out of us."

But as he advanced deeper into his presidency, Obama played less basketball and more golf (see "The Inevitability of Golf," page 107). The change could be traced in part to the November 2010 incident in which he needed twelve

After ignoring the first pass of the Verizon Center Kiss Cam during a July 2012 U.S. men's national team exhibition against Brazil, the First Couple give the crowd what it wants when the camera comes around again. (Pete Souza/The White House.) Inset: (Leslie E. Kossoff/Pool/Corbis/AP Images.)

stitches after taking an elbow to the mouth during a game at Fort McNair (see "Lip Service," page 90). As one of his frequent golfing partners, Alonzo Mourning, put it, "He didn't want to do the State of the Union speech on crutches or with a broken nose."

Watching their exemplar drift away from the game, basketball partisans fretted openly. When Obama's political fortunes ebbed—as they did during his most politically challenging year, 2014, when he hardly played at all—these supporters argued that he would find a panacea in the sport of his youth if he would only return to it. "The fact that he isn't playing . . . is a metaphor for those people who think he's gotten soft, backed off his promises, sold out," said Claude Johnson. "When President Obama goes back to basketball, that will be a sign that we haven't lost the original guy."

Edward Alden, an analyst at the Council on Foreign Relations, went so far as to suggest, in a *Washington Post* op-ed shortly after Democratic losses in the 2014 midterms, that golf had worked a kind of juju on the president. "Like basketball, politics is a blood sport. If you want to play, you risk getting hurt. Otherwise, you should do something else. . . . So, please, Mr. President. For all of us, quit the links and get back on the court."

In fact, out of the public eye, he had taken to the court in a different capacity—as a coach of the Vipers, his daughter Sasha's team in a Montgomery County (Maryland) girls' league. The president and his assistant coach, Love, couldn't make every game, but they turned up at Saturday morning practices as often as they could to lead the team through drills. White House personnel loved one of Souza's photos, never released to the public, in which Obama falls in among the fourth-grade girls, just another body in sync. Even as president, Obama could serve Sasha and her teammates in a role that his own father had never been around to fill. "The girls, they just think of it as dad," he said. "This is what dads are supposed to do."

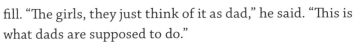

In the basement gym at Interior Department headquarters, a couple of blocks from the White House, the "extremely lefthanded" president works on his right hand with daughters Sasha (*left*) and Malia. (Pete Souza/The White House.)

As a youth coach, Obama was less stem-winding motivator than technocrat. He wouldn't let the Vipers practice three-pointers because he knew they wouldn't be shooting from a distance during a game. Instead he drilled them in the pick and roll. "You just want them to win so bad," he said. "And when they actually run a play and it works, you're just ecstatic. And a couple of heartbreaking losses and you're just feeling terrible."

With his recreational basketball career subordinate to Sasha's, in 2012 Obama scaled back the Election Day gathering from the festival of four years before. Once again participants converged on Attack Athletics in Chicago, but this time for one game between two teams, led by player-coaches Obama and Chicago buddy Marty Nesbitt. The reversible jerseys now read "4 MORE YEARS," and certified officials in striped shirts worked the game, which Obama's team wound up winning by 12. (Team Obama included Hall of Famer Scottie Pippen, who took to the court despite a medial collateral ligament tear, vowing, "I'm not gonna miss *this*.") The smaller group stood felicitously for the more intimate circle into which presidents tend to retreat as their time in office wears on.

When he was entirely alone, Obama could still find in the game a virtual companion, thanks to ESPN. Monitors would be tuned to *SportsCenter* during his early-morning workouts. "I can't sit down and watch an entire game, except maybe the Super Bowl or the NBA Finals or the World Series," he said. "But there are times, I will admit, at night when I've got a really fat briefing book, I might have a game on with the sound off."

Cable and satellite carriers that served the D.C. market picked up word of the president's late-night viewing habits. Soon sales staffs had done their work, and in the wee hours you could find issue ads dropped into ESPN programming, some advocating for gun laws, others against fossil fuels, all targeted at an audience of one.

Facing page: The president and personal aide Reggie Love usually confined their guest coaching of Sasha Obama's youth league team to practices. But when the regular coaches couldn't make this game, in February 2011, the two threw themselves enthusiastically into the breach. (Pete Souza/The White House.)

Baracketology

For the first seven Marches of his presidency, Barack Obama spent the Tuesday before the start of the NCAA men's basketball tournament very publicly filling out his brackets. Those picks, revealed with ESPN's Andy Katz and posted like any policy statement on WhiteHouse.gov, touched off curiosity, punditry, and occasional controversy.

Analysts had their opinions. Obama's tendency to pick the chalk was emblematic of his cautious nature. He had blundered by ignoring the women's bracket, an oversight he acknowledged by sharing his women's picks with Katz's colleagues Rebecca Lobo or Doris Burke every March after that first. The mere fact that he chose to devote time to the exercise was scandalous, majority whip Kevin McCarthy (R-Calif.)

. . . .

Facing page: ESPN's Andy Katz visited the White House every March to unveil the presidential bracket (inset). Obama, joined in the larger photo by aides (*from left*) Robert Gibbs, David Axelrod, and Reggie Love, follows his picks. (Pete Souza/The White House.)

charged, when the White House hadn't yet delivered a budget. (A typical Fox News chyron, from 2014: "OBAMA PICKS NCAA BRACKET WHILE PUTIN DECLARES CRIMEA AS PART OF RUSSIA.") As for the deep runs he foretold for teams in swing states—before he was safely reelected, that's where half of the teams to make his Final Fours came from—wasn't that what you'd expect from a politician? "A complete coincidence," Obama told Jay Leno over laughter on *The Tonight Show*. Data guru Nate Silver nonetheless reverse-engineered Obama's 2009 bracket with what he called "a logistic regression model" and concluded that the president's picks did indeed have a swing-state bias.

As it happened, "Baracketology" could be traced to a seemingly unrelated figure: retired general Colin Powell. During the 2008 campaign, to balance an ESPN *Outside the Lines* segment about Cindy McCain's passion for auto racing, Katz pitched a piece looking into Obama's connection to basketball, including the role his brother-in-law, Oregon State coach Craig Robinson, played in the senator's decision to run. Two

Sundays before Election Day, Katz and an ESPN crew caught up with the campaign at a Hampton Inn in Dunn, North Carolina, near Fort Bragg, where Obama was scheduled to speak. As Obama sat for the interview that morning, advisor David Axelrod and press secretary Robert Gibbs got word that Powell had just endorsed their candidate on *Meet the Press*. The news meant that Obama would need to revise his prepared remarks. But until Axelrod and Gibbs could discuss exactly how, the candidate wouldn't be leaving that Hampton Inn—and Katz suddenly found himself with forty extra minutes.

"Now, we're just talking," Katz recalled. "And I say, 'Senator, if you win, how about I come to the White House and fill out the bracket with you?' He says, 'Sure.' And I turn to Axelrod and Gibbs and say, 'You heard that?' And they say, 'Yeah, yeah.'"

At that, Katz's producer leaned over and whispered to him, "You realize, you may have just invited yourself to the White House."

Katz clinched the deal during the transition. And as members of the ESPN delegation left the White House that first year, lugging away a marked-up whiteboard graced with the presidential seal, they found themselves trailed by two *Politico* reporters desperate for a peek at Obama's picks.

In 2011 the filming nearly didn't take place. Katz later learned that, earlier in the day, Obama had met to plan the raid that would kill Osama bin Laden. "In retrospect, I could tell," Katz said. "He was into [the tournament], he knew it, but he was a little rushed." Days earlier, a tsunami had hit the Japanese coast; at the request of the White House, ESPN turned the unveiling of the bracket into a kind of public service announcement, flashing a phone number for donations on the screen.

"When it first started, Republicans were critical," Katz said. "Rush Limbaugh was taking shots and there was a feeding frenzy on Fox." But by Obama's second term the practice had jumped the aisle, as politicians of all stripes tried to bond with their respective electorates. GOP senators Rob Portman of Ohio, Rand Paul of Kentucky, and Marco Rubio of Florida began to make public their brackets or predictions. In 2015, joining Katz

in the Rotunda of Congress, Paul Ryan (R-Wisc.) talked up his home-state Badgers and Cathy McMorris Rodgers (R-Wash.) touted Gonzaga, which sits in her district. At the same time, presidential hopeful Jeb Bush was pushing out on social media a full bracket, as if it were some position paper. Indeed, 2015 was the year much of the world accepted that the president would fill out a bracket, and instead used his picks for validation or motivation. "The fuck wrong with Barack Obama?" said North Carolina State's Anthony (Cat) Barber in the locker room after the Wolfpack, the president's pick as second-round losers to Villanova, upset the Wildcats. Brenda Frese, coach of the top-seeded Maryland women, was less profane but just as eager to rub it in the First Fan's face. "Sorry, man, but we had to bust your bracket!" she said in the locker room after her Terps ruined Obama's upset special, Princeton—whereupon her players pummeled a cardboard cutout of the president, who had at least owned up to a bias because his niece played for the Tigers. Confirmation that Baracketology had

become part of the natural order, in official Washington and beyond, also came in 2015, when ESPN delivered that year's presidential bracket boards to the Smithsonian. They were placed in storage for possible inclusion in a future exhibit about how American culture gives rise to shared experiences.

During the 2012 campaign Katz was asked if he would continue to do the brackets with a President Romney. "There'd be an obligation to ask out of bipartisanship," he said. "But we probably wouldn't do it if he didn't follow the sport." In March 2012, asked for his own picks, Romney confessed, "I'm not plugged in well enough" to do a bracket. (Three years later Romney entered the ESPN Tournament Challenge—and placed in the 99.9th percentile.)

Said Katz, "With [George W.] Bush, if you did a baseball bracket, he'd hit it out of the park. With Obama, this has worked for the same reason—because he's interested."

The White House decided it made sense to project the president's basketball brand beyond that of a pickup player. "I don't think anyone will be elected president by filling out an NCAA bracket," said Axelrod. "But I do think that that accessibility to a person is important. People want to support people they can relate to and are comfortable with."

Indeed, Obama was filling out a bracket long before ESPN's cameras began documenting his picks. That first year, after choosing North Carolina as his champion, he turned to address the camera. "The Tar Heels that are watchin', I picked you all last year and you let me down," he said. "This year, don't embarrass me in front of the nation, all right? I'm counting on you."

They didn't embarrass him. For the only time during seven years in the White House, Obama's pick to win it all actually did. ∎

Hardwood Cabinet

Playground rhetoric sometimes makes for over-the-top bravado, but Barack Obama surely did assemble what in 2009 he called "the best basketball-playing cabinet in American history." Among the group, Secretary of Education Arne Duncan (page 85) continued to play at a remarkably high level, even while in office. Obama's brother-in-law Craig Robinson (page 31) was an NBA draft pick, and personal aide Reggie Love (page 46) won an NCAA title at Duke. But hoop savvy extended to a broad range of people close to the president, including allies on Capitol Hill and longtime friends. Here is a survey of basketball characters in the White House orbit during Obama's two terms.

David Axelrod
Political Strategist and Senior Advisor
He met his wife-to-be, Susan Landau, while playing in a regular coed pickup game in Chicago's Hyde Park during the seventies. . . . At the time Susan was dating another regular in the game, but four years later she and David began to see each other. . . . A longtime Bulls season-ticket holder, he was also a self-described "occasional caboose on the train" during campaign pickup games, where he was notorious for his streaky outside shooting.

Joe Biden
Vice President
Served as manager of the freshman team at Archmere Academy in Claymont, Delaware. . . . He tossed in a shot from beyond half-court during a 2008 visit to a school in Iowa. . . . His Secret Service code name during that campaign was Celtic. . . . His granddaughter Maisy played on the same Maryland girls' youth league team as Sasha Obama.

Sen. Robert Casey
Democrat from Pennsylvania
A self-described "banger" at Scranton (Pennsylvania) Prep, he was an early Obama supporter who forged a bond with the candidate during pickup games while campaigning across Pennsylvania. . . . His father played freshman ball at Holy Cross, scrimmaging against future Celtics Tom Heinsohn and Bob Cousy. . . . He

Power, Forward

77

Sen. Robert Casey. (Adam Wells—Office of Sen. Robert Casey.)

was among the thirty-five people who participated in the 2008 Election Day game in Chicago.

Timothy Geithner
Secretary of the Treasury
While president of the Federal Reserve Bank of New York, he played in its rec league. . . . During a 2010 visit to China's Renmin University, Geithner jumped into a half-court scrimmage with the school team, sinking a three-pointer despite wearing suit pants and a button-down shirt. . . . At 5′8″, he

was cut twice and served as manager before making his high school team, but his father, Pete, captained Dartmouth during the fifties and tried out for the Celtics.

Julius Genachowski
Chair of the Federal Communications Commission
As a colleague of Obama's on the *Harvard Law Review,* he would join Obama for pickup games in Hemenway Gym, adjacent to the magazine's offices. . . . During the nineties, as a clerk for Supreme Court justices William Brennan and David Souter, he played daily on the court above the judges' chambers, a.k.a. "the highest court in the land."

Alexi Giannoulias
Illinois State Treasurer
Elected to statewide office at age twenty-eight with Obama's support. . . . The two met in pickup games at the University of Chicago, where Giannoulias was a graduate student and the future president a Law School lecturer. . . . As a 6′2″ guard, starred at Boston University and played a season in Greece for Panionios. . . . In a May

2008 pickup game, he bruised the candidate's ribs while driving on him, causing Obama to black out.

Hill Harper
Television Actor
The star of *CSI: NY* attended Harvard Law School, where he met Obama and regularly played with him. . . . Harper, a 5′9″ high school football star in the Bay Area, organized a late-eighties pickup game between members of the Black Law Students Association and inmates at a maximum security prison in Walpole, Massachusetts, in which Obama participated. . . .

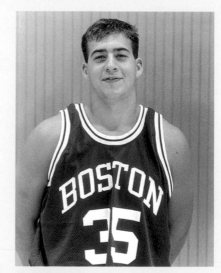

Alexi Giannoulias. (Boston University Photo Services.)

A member of Obama's campaign finance committee, he also took part in the 2008 Election Day run in Chicago.

Eric Holder
Attorney General

A 6′2″ native of Queens and co-captain at Manhattan's Stuyvesant High, he played a season of freshman ball at Columbia. . . . "In a school of short academic nerds," a Stuyvesant teammate recalled, "he was a tall academic nerd." . . . Asked during his confirmation hearings by Sen. Herb Kohl (D-Wisc.), the owner of the Milwaukee Bucks, if he could beat Obama one-on-one, Holder replied, "He's 10 years younger than me. He plays a lot more frequently than I do. Having said that, I've got a New York City game. . . . If you give me a little time to get back in shape, I think I can hang with him."

Retired General James Jones
National Security Advisor

For two seasons between 1963 and 1965, the future Supreme Allied Commander Europe came off the bench as a 6′4″ frontcourt rebounder for Georgetown. . . . Even into his sixties, the former Hoya was known for his versatility and soft touch. . . . He once credited the game with preparing him for a career in the Marines, where he had to both take orders and make on-the-fly decisions himself.

Janet Napolitano
Director of Homeland Security

The former Arizona governor served as guest or honorary coach for the WNBA's Phoenix Mercury as well as women's teams at Arizona and Arizona State. . . . The Mercury, Wildcats, and Sun Devils all won with her on bench, giving "Coach Nap" a lifetime unblemished record. . . . She once asked her orthopedist to wrap a broken ankle in orange and purple bandages, to show support for her favorite NBA team, the Phoenix Suns.

Marty Nesbitt
Chicago Businessman and Obama Campaign Treasurer

He got to know Obama through Craig Robinson and while participating in

Janet Napolitano (*far right*). (AP Photo/John Miller.)

Marty Nesbitt. (Courtesy of Albion College.)

Chicago pickup games. . . . Played at Division III Albion College in Michigan, where he served as co-captain. . . . As "commissioner" for Obama's Election Day games, Nesbitt helped the president draw up teams. . . . In 2013 he and Kip Kirkpatrick, a former player at Northwestern, founded a private equity firm. . . . A son, Alex, played in the backcourt for Harvard.

Marvin Nicholson

Campaign and White House Travel Director

A 6'8" Canadian American with limited mobility, he played ball at the University of Western Ontario. . . .

He had been John Kerry's Reggie Love during the 2004 campaign before signing on with Obama to head up travel. . . . Though frequently conscripted to play basketball, he was best known for having played golf with Obama some 140 times through September 2014, more often than anyone else.

Greg Orme and Mike Ramos

Fellow Students at Punahou School in Honolulu

Two members of the "band of brothers" to haunt the courts of Oahu with the future president as the young Obama came of age. . . . Orme went on to join him on Punahou's 1979 state title team, and like Ramos continued to play into adulthood. . . . The two flew in for Election Day games in Chicago and reunited regularly over the Christmas holidays in Hawaii, often playing ball with Obama.

Dan Pfeiffer

White House Communications Director and Senior Advisor

At Wilmington (Delaware) Friends School, he was a 6'2" forward. . . . He played pickup ball regularly and

attended the games of his alma mater, Georgetown, as well as D.C. high school match-ups of note. . . . When Sen. Mitch McConnell (R-Ky.) attributed a rebounding economy in late 2014 to "the expectation of a new Republican Congress," Pfeiffer invoked Stacey King's 1990 comment after Chicago Bulls teammate Michael Jordan scored sixty-nine points: "I'll always remember this as the night that Michael Jordan and I combined for 70 points."

Dan Pfeiffer. (Courtesy of Wilmington Friends School.)

Samantha Power

Ambassador to the United Nations

Her UN office included a basketball signed by Obama with the inscription, "You will always be my MVP." . . . At Lakeside High School in Atlanta, she won eleven varsity letters but "loved basketball the best." . . . Once played pickup ball with actor George Clooney, who joined her as an advocate for a muscular response to the genocide in Darfur. . . . She occasionally played at the Interior Department, where at 5′9″ she was known as "The Tower of Power." . . . As an undergraduate at Yale she co-hosted a sports talk show on the student radio station.

Susan Rice
Ambassador to the United Nations and National Security Advisor
A 5′3″ point guard at the National Cathedral School in D.C., where she picked up the nickname "Spo," short for "Sportin'." . . . She played on the New College team at Oxford during a year spent there as a Rhodes Scholar. . . . Her brother, John, a former NBA marketing executive, played at Yale and regularly took part in the president's full-court games.

John Rogers
Chicago Businessman and Co-chair of Obama's Inauguration Committees
A teammate of Craig Robinson's at Princeton, where he captained the Tigers in 1979–1980. . . . He participated in the pickup game

Susan Rice (*center*). (Courtesy of National Cathedral School.)

John Rogers. (Photo by W. L. Bill Allen Jr.—NJSportAction.NET.)

at which Robinson vetted Obama as a potential brother-in-law. . . . The motto of his business, Ariel Investments, is "Slow and steady wins the race," which also describes his own hoop style—and which he once used to beat Michael Jordan in a game of one-on-one. . . . Robinson and Arne Duncan joined him to win national three-on-three tournaments for Team Ariel.

Ken Salazar
Secretary of the Interior

During the former Colorado senator's four years in the cabinet, the basketball court at the Interior Department became the site of a game featuring ex–campaign workers and younger White House aides. . . . In 2009 Salazar, a tough defender who once played in a Greater Denver men's league, challenged Obama to come use the court. . . . Several weeks later the president did, beating an Interior team with his White House crew.

Paul Volcker
Chair of the Economic Recovery Advisory Board

A 6'7" center at Teaneck (New Jersey) High, the former chairman of the Federal Reserve was eighty-one when he accepted Obama's call to help pull the country out of the Great Recession. . . . A substitute at Princeton, he has said that he didn't get along with the coach. . . . Of his days as a Tiger, he once said, "It was a major event when I got into a game."

Paul Volcker. (Courtesy of Princeton University.)

Dr. Eric Whitaker
Executive Vice President of the University of Chicago Medical Center

Met the future president and bonded with him over basketball at Harvard, where Obama attended law school and Whitaker earned a master's in public health. . . . Played at Division III Grinnell College in Iowa. . . . "When you come up through the elite schools there's not

Dr. Eric Whitaker (*left*). (Courtesy of Grinnell College Libraries Archives & Special Collections.)

a lot of diversity, and the basketball court was one place where you could bond and find black men," he said.

Mary Jo White
Chair of the Securities and Exchange Commission

Though only 5 feet tall, she was an avid pickup player as a U.S. Attorney in New York during the seventies and joined several women on a rec-league team. . . . "People checked their knees for teeth marks," said a lawyer who played with her. . . . "The same toughness she shows playing basketball she will show as SEC chair," said Sen. Charles Schumer (D-N.Y.) at her 2013 confirmation hearings. "She will score many points and commit few fouls."■

The Secretary of Schoolin' People

Arne Duncan's relationship to basketball could be reduced to a gag line like the one above. Or it could be passed off as a collection of trivia, each item capable on its own of raising an eyebrow. Barack Obama's 6'5" secretary of education, a former co-captain at Harvard, played with 5'3" Muggsy Bogues for the USBL's Rhode Island Gulls. He earned the nickname the Cobra during four seasons as a professional in Australia. He helped Michael Jordan play back into shape for his 2001 comeback with the Washington Wizards. He had a cameo in *Benji,* the ESPN *30-for-30* documentary about slain Chicago high school star Ben Wilson, as the white guy in the background of game footage. And talk about your common core: As a Hoop-It-Up three-on-three

. . . .

Facing page: Secretary of Education Arne Duncan jumps into a game at a Haitian lycée in the Port-au-Prince suburb of Pétionville. Duncan and USAID announced an educational aid package during his 2013 visit to the Caribbean nation. (AP Photo/Dieu Nalio Chery.)

player between 2003 and 2014, he won nine of eleven possible national championships, including three with Obama insiders and former Princeton players Craig Robinson and John Rogers.

But there was nothing random about Duncan's achievements during 2014, when he pulled off a triple that would have been impressive for someone of any age, much less a forty-nine-year-old whose job had him traveling constantly. In addition to that Hoop-It-Up title, he won the MVP trophy in the Celebrity Game at NBA All-Star Weekend, scoring twenty points, grabbing eleven rebounds, and dishing out six assists, including a highlight that went viral on the web—a blind flip to a cutting Skylar Diggins for a layup. Three months later, playing for Chicago-based, Rogers-sponsored Team Ariel, he joined recent Princeton center Mack Darrow and former Northwestern players Jitim Young and Craig Moore to win USA Basketball's national three-on-three championship. The title qualified Team Ariel for the FIBA 3x3 Worlds in Russia, a country with which the

government Duncan served was then in bitter conflict over Moscow's invasion of Ukraine. Duncan had to bow out because of a packed schedule—"Commencement season," he said—and no time to rearrange it in the short window before the competition. "He was heartbroken," Rogers said. "To miss out on a chance to represent his country. . . . I've never heard Arne more sad than when he realized he couldn't go."

But the point had been made: Here was no typical cabinet official. Even on the cusp of his fifties, Duncan remained the beau ideal of a pickup teammate. "He played with relaxed ferocity, combining opportunistic defense with slashing moves to the basket, shrewd passes, and feathery hesitation jumpers," reported Carlo Rotella, a high school classmate of Duncan's at the University of Chicago Lab School, after playing in a noontime run with him in 2009. "He attended to the finer points of the game with a contagious virtue."

Though the son of two white educators, Duncan grew up under racially ambiguous circumstances, much like the president he served.

From the time Arne was a toddler, his mother, Sue, took him with her to the after-school tutoring center she ran in a church basement in the North Kenwood–Oakland neighborhood on Chicago's South Side. Sue Duncan sometimes had to face down local gangs; one firebombed that church basement after the pastor refused a demand that it be used instead as an arsenal. Duncan, then six, remembers the aftermath, carrying salvaged books to another church down the block.

Duncan essentially grew up at "the Sue," bonding with local kids over basketball, sometimes relying on nonverbal communication, the academic specialty of his father, Starkey, a University of Chicago psychology professor. Even years later, when he did speak, Arne retained the inflections of the neighborhood so thoroughly that at least one college coach, hanging up after a recruiting call, would assume he was black.

By the time he hit his teens, Duncan had already wandered from the tutoring center to a playground across the street. Soon he began to play farther afield, including once on a court across from a crack house. "It was an extraordinary experience, not just to develop as a ballplayer, but to learn whom to trust and how to survive," Duncan said. "When stuff happened, I knew how to get out and get out quick. Obviously I was the outsider, and guys on the streets frankly protected me. To this day, I owe my life to them. The community never let us down."

He never called "next" on a South Side court. "Somebody always set me up," he said. "Some were kids from the neighborhood who made me a little brother and some of them were gang leaders I didn't know that well. I remember there was a guy named Cabbage. I didn't even know his real name, just Cabbage."

Duncan won broad respect as much for his even temper as for his game. Rogers remembered the day a fight broke out in a South Side gym. "Arne waded in like a referee does, and one of the guys punched him," he recalled. "The gym went silent. They got that guy out of there. There were like threats on his life, because he'd punched Arne."

Duncan arrived at Harvard in 1982 lightly recruited and looking very Obamaesque—6'2", scrawny, left-handed. He averaged thirty points a game for the jayvee, then made the varsity after sprouting three inches over the following summer. Before his senior season he took a year off and returned to Chicago, to study why some ghetto kids make it and others don't. Using his mother's tutoring center as a base, he carved out time to coach and play between stretches of teaching, mentoring, and interviewing. His findings wound up in a senior thesis, "The Values, Aspirations and Opportunities of the Urban Underclass," for Harvard's Sociology Department, which awarded him a B.A. magna cum laude.

In Cambridge, the Harvard coaches noticed, Duncan would never call a foul during pickup games. To call one, remembered Steve Bzomowski, then a Crimson assistant along with future Chicago Bulls coach Tom Thibodeau, was "an excuse he did not want to use. Excuses equated to failure, and he just did not see things that way." If Duncan as cabinet secretary seemed impatient when some stakeholder in the world of education invoked an extenuating circumstance, perhaps it was just another example of his longtime aversion to excuses.

"Arne Duncan was not a great talent, but boy, did he understand and see deep into the game," Bzomowski added. "I think he believed in the game and in his belief that he could be very, very good at it even while others might not have thought so. Isn't that what great teachers, what great educators possess? The unwavering belief that their pupils can and should and will succeed."

In 2010 Duncan took the NCAA itself to school. He used a speech at the organization's annual convention to rip colleges that failed to graduate more players, especially African American ones, in revenue-producing sports. His remarks resonated with an understanding of life on the far side of Forty-Seventh Street, the dividing line between the world he had come home to each evening as a child and the one in which he had spent his afternoons. A year later, when the NCAA tightened its minimum graduation standards for a school to maintain postseason eligibility, Duncan knew he had been heard.

"This stuff is very personal to me," he said. "I grew up playing with guys who never graduated college, never made the NBA, never made a nickel. They were on national TV, making millions for their universities, and now they're back on the streets, hustling and playing with me. As a teenager, that got seared into my mind. To me, enriching universities and coaches and sponsors and TV, with nothing in return on the academic side, is morally unacceptable." ∎

. . . .

Duncan posts up Reggie Love during a game at the Interior Department gym. Marty Nesbitt, one of Obama's Chicago-based friends, looks to get an entry pass past the president. (Pete Souza/The White House.)

Center Circles

Pickup basketball enjoyed standing in official Washington long before Barack Obama took up residence in the White House. Since the forties, law clerks and even a few Supreme Court justices had gone at it on "the highest court in the land," on the fifth floor of the Supreme Court, except when court was in session, lest bouncing balls reverberate in the chambers below. The gym in the Interior Department's basement, a short walk from the White House, also got heavy use. Regulars at the Dupont Circle Y accustomed to playing with "the tall guy named Mark," as one of them called him, did a double-take one day when Mark Warner wound up as governor of Virginia. And for years, in the sub-basement of the Rayburn House Office Building, a.k.a.

Facing page: A game involving the president made for the most intimate of inner circles in Obama-era Washington. Here presidential aide Reggie Love beats members of Congress, cabinet officials, and administration aides down the floor as POTUS watches from the backcourt. (Pete Souza/The White House.)

the House gym, Rep. Tom Downey (D-N.Y.) presided over a game featuring such congressmen as Mike Oxley (R-Ohio), Al Gore (D-Tenn.), Rod Chandler (R-Wash.), and Ed Markey (D-Mass.). There in Room SB-322 you might find John Boehner (R-Ohio) sneaking a smoke on the sideline; or Pat Roberts (R-Kan.) setting picks that once knocked two teeth from a distinguished colleague's mouth; or Sen. Bill Bradley (D-N.J.) making a rare inter-chamber cameo when the Hall of Famer needed to corral House votes for his 1986 tax reform bill. With the game tipping off at 4 P.M., Speaker Tip O'Neill (D-Mass.) promised not to hold votes in the late afternoon out of respect for "the Four O'Clock Caucus," or Members' Basketball Association—the MBA.

But nothing would jolt the city's sleepy pickup scene more suddenly than the arrival of a president who regularly laced 'em up. Rep. Baron Hill (D-Ind.), a star at Seymour (Indiana) High School and a member of the Indiana Basketball Hall of Fame, wasn't too proud to admit in June 2009 why, at fifty-five, he was getting back into game shape: "If I

ever have an opportunity to play with him, I want to be able to halfway get around that court well enough." With Obama's arrival, even that old game in the House gym, which by 2006 had faded away, wheezed back to life, this time as an early-morning run with Rep. Heath Shuler (D-N.C.), the former University of Tennessee and Washington Redskins quarterback, in charge.

"That first year or two there was definitely a buzz around the city and the basketball community," said Arthur Jackson, a former player at Brown whose D.C. coaching firm, One-on-One Basketball, saw a steady rise in business around Obama's 2009 inauguration. "A little bit of it was people dusting off their jump shots. Who wouldn't want to play with the President?"

Or as Bill Clinton's former press secretary, DeeDee Myers, put it, a pickup game with Obama was "the inner, inner, inner sanctum. Proximity is everything in this town."

Beyond the anglers trying to worm their way into a game to make connections, basketball became the sport to which Washington's power parents steered their kids. "We went from 60 teams to 120 to more than 300," said Jackson, whose company organized youth leagues for children aged five and up. "And [by 2013] we had over 800 teams in our leagues. You'd walk in the gym and see Eric Holder, Arne Duncan, Susan Rice, big-time lobbyists—all their kids, playing basketball, and they're just normal parents at the game."

If you could really play and had a connection, you wouldn't bother with some second-order game lousy with junior aides or GS-12s. A much more rarified orbital awaited: the Saturday morning run at which Obama, Love, Duncan, and others turned up. Aside from the occasional media interloper like *Vanity Fair*'s Michael Lewis, virtually everyone in the gym other than the Secret Service

agents and the national security aide with the nuclear football had high-level high school or some college experience. "Every time I've played, Reggie isn't on the President's team," said Jackson. "And Arne is *always* on his team. The President is very competitive, and there was definitely a Reggie-President competition going on."

The Saturday morning game may have been the toughest. But it was also the purest, because no one harbored any motive beyond wanting to play hard and well. As Secretary of Transportation Ray LaHood told cast members of the MTV reality series *The Buried Life,* who came through D.C. in 2009 looking for a game with Obama, "Are you guys really legit basketball players? Because they don't mess around down there."∎

Lip Service

On November 26, 2010, the Friday after Thanksgiving, the ballplayers who gathered at the gym at D.C.'s Fort McNair, POTUS included, had turkey to work off. But they wouldn't complete their final game that morning, not after Barack Obama took an elbow to the mouth from a thirty-eight-year-old Washingtonian named Rey Decerega.

After emigrating with his family from Panama as a six-year-old, Decerega had found that basketball played much the same role in his life as it had in Obama's—as a way to fit in. Twice Decerega won state titles at St. Stephen's School of Alexandria, Virginia, and over summers he haunted greater D.C. Boys and Girls Clubs and playgrounds. At the University of Virginia he played intramurals, and after graduating with a degree in history he became a schoolteacher and coach before landing at the Congressional Hispanic Caucus Institute as its director of leadership programs.

Decerega had played with the president once before, at Camp

David, where Obama made a point of chatting him up. The two spoke briefly about what they had in common: tasting a state championship in high school and remaining devoted Basketball Bennies after having organized careers cut short. "It almost creates a chip on your shoulder," Decerega said. "It's a chapter in your life that's never fully written, because it wasn't explored further or circumstances wouldn't allow it."

Decerega had been Obama's teammate that day at Camp David, and made a favorable enough impression to be invited back to the fateful run at Fort McNair. The post-Thanksgiving game was much like the first, with many of the same characters (presidential aide Reggie Love; Secretary of Education Arne Duncan; former Yale guard John Rice, brother of Susan Rice, then Obama's ambassador to the United Nations)

. . . .

The president leaves Fort McNair with a Secret Service agent in November 2010 after the abrupt end of a Friday-morning game. An inadvertent elbow opened a cut on his lip that required a dozen stitches to close. (AP Photo/Charles Dharapak.)

and exactly the same vibe. "It was competitive," Decerega recalled. "Nobody was backing down, which is what happens if you're programmed to play a certain way."

Four games went off without incident. "The President said, 'Let's play another,'" recalled Arthur

Jackson, a former player at Brown who had worked with Love to organize the game. "On the first play the President made a great move along the baseline and scored. And on the very next play, it happened."

Obama, adrenaline likely pumping after that artful basket, threw up

his hands and crowded Decerega on defense. Decerega swung the ball instinctively from right to left, trying to clear space. That's when Decerega's right elbow struck Obama in the mouth, opening up a gash on his lip that would require a dozen small-filament stitches to close.

"Time stood still," Jackson recalled. "We knew that, O.K., today's game was over."

"The fact that you elbow the President of the United States is so hard to fathom," said Decerega, who needed four stitches of his own to close the wound on his elbow.

From that day forward, the president played with a mouth guard.

When Love called later that day to check in, Decerega pleaded with him to keep his identity secret. That, Love explained, was no longer an option. "The press is hounding us about this," he said. "They're already calling it Elbowgate."

Decerega worked with the White House to prepare a brief statement. Reporters nonetheless doorstepped his home, and e-mails popped into his inbox from both Obama partisans who called him racist and Obama haters who chided him for not swinging harder.

To help him come to terms with the episode, Decerega wrote the president a note of apology. Three days later he received in the mail a framed, photographic triptych of the sequence—Obama playing tight defense, Decerega swinging through with the ball, the president clutching his bloody lip—as captured by official White House photographer Pete Souza. "For Rey," the inscription read. "The only guy that ever hit the president and never got arrested. Barack."

"The elbow happened," Decerega said. "But when the package came I felt a level of relief. I was just playing hard, and he recognized that. I think he respected good old-fashioned competition and that this was an accident. His gift of that photograph was a gesture of kindness. But I think it was also his way of saying, 'It was just a game.'"■

Ding-Dong Diplomacy

After years of tensions with North Korea, Barack Obama took the oath of office in 2009 willing to revisit America's relationship with that impenetrable country. But four months into his presidency Pyongyang violated a nuclear test ban, a move that turned anyone in the White House not already a hawk on North Korea into one. That's where relations between the countries stood—stalemated, with belligerent rhetoric on one side and an anxious wariness on the other—when Hall of Famer Dennis Rodman made his way to the Hermit Kingdom.

The former Chicago Bull and Detroit Piston touched down in Pyongyang in February 2013 wearing an earring, a nose ring, a lip piercing, and, if it could be discerned beneath a black USA Basketball cap, a hairstyle presumably not among the ten officially sanctioned by the regime. During four trips to North Korea over an eleven-month span, including one with several Harlem Globetrotters in tow, Rodman called ruler Kim Jong-un "my friend for life"; serenaded him at a private dinner with a rendition of Sinatra's "My Way"; celebrated the dictator's thirty-first birthday by joining seven other former NBA players (Kenny Anderson, Vin Baker, Charles Smith, Sleepy Floyd, Cliff Robinson, Doug Christie, and Craig Hodges) in an exhibition game against a North Korean side; and asked Kim to "do me a solid" by releasing Kenneth Bae, a Korean American missionary who had been sentenced to fifteen years of hard labor on charges of trying to overthrow the regime. "His whole deal is to talk basketball with Obama," Rodman said. "Unfortunately, Obama doesn't want to have anything to do with him. I ask, Mr. President, what's the harm in a simple phone call? This is a new age, man. Come on, Obama, reach out to Kim and be his friend."

Human rights groups blanched. They pointed out North Korea's work camps, summary executions, and hundreds of thousands of political prisoners. A State Department spokesman criticized the regime for "wining and dining" Rodman while its own people starved. If anything, Rodman seemed to be setting relations back; two weeks before his first visit, Pyongyang tested another nuclear warhead, and even after the Rodman démarche, the regime ratcheted up its bluster. "Settling accounts with the U.S. needs to be done with force, not with words," vowed the government, which pledged "a new phase of the anti-U.S. struggle that has lasted century after century."

"Before I landed in Pyongyang, I didn't know Kim Jong-un from Lil' Kim," the five-time NBA Champion confessed. "I didn't know what country he ruled or what went on in the country he ruled." But basketball had become entwined with U.S.–North Korean relations long before the Worm's first visit. In 1991 the State Department hosted a North Korean delegation led by a Kim Jong-il confidante who insisted on watching NBA games in the evenings, something this emissary said he would do back home "with the boss." The delegation's host, Foggy Bottom Korea specialist Eugene Schmiel, was so taken by his guest's enthusiasm for the game that he made note of it in a diplomatic memo, suggesting that basketball, like Ping-Pong before it, might be grounds for a breakthrough.

In May 1997 Pyongyang sent a North Korean citizen, 7′9″ Ri Myong Hun, to Canada to work out in front of NBA scouts. Even though Ri was by all accounts a legitimate pro prospect, the State Department vowed to block any contract under the Trading with the Enemy Act. But that December, during nuclear arms talks in Geneva, the United States seemed to have a change of heart. Negotiators broached the possibility of Ri playing in the NBA as an inducement for Pyongyang to sign a nonproliferation agreement. The use of Ri as a bargaining chip so infuriated Kim that he ordered his seven-footer, who now used the name Michael Ri in honor of Michael Jordan, to return home. "It was absurd that we didn't pick up on that signal and give a visa to that player," said Robert Carlin, who was then a State Department intelligence analyst focused on North Korea. "Basketball could have been used more adroitly."

But the Kim family's interest in the NBA persisted. When they were students at a Swiss boarding school during the late nineties, the young Kim Jong-un would make pencil sketches of Jordan and wear the eponymous Nike shoe, while his brother, Kim Jong-chul, walked around campus in a Rodman No. 91 Bulls jersey. In 2000 Secretary of State Madeleine Albright, during the first visit of any senior American official to Pyongyang, gave their father a Jordan-autographed basketball that quickly found a place in the country's Museum of International Understanding.

When Bae was released in November 2014 after serving thirty-one months, Rodman produced a letter he had written to Kim the previous January, pleading with the Supreme Leader to let Bae go. It seemed at least possible that the hands once so adept at snaring rebounds had actually helped secure Bae's release.

Were Rodman's carny-barking visits lost opportunities, oafish deployments of "the hoop card"? Or will they someday be looked back on as an opening in relations between the two governments? "I don't think by itself basketball would have built a relationship, but it wouldn't have been a bad plank in the platform," says Carlin, who was captivated by video of the Globetrotters placing spinning basketballs on the fingers of delighted children. "There was something there. Apart from the Leader liking basketball, North Koreans themselves like it. At one point during Rodman's visit, Americans and North Koreans played on the same team. That and the Leader sitting next to an American are pretty powerful symbols. So there might be something for a future administration to go back to."∎

....

Facing page: Dennis Rodman and North Korean supreme leader Kim Jong-un watch a game between the host country and a delegation of former NBA players at Pyongyang Indoor Stadium in January 2014. Rodman made his visit to the Hermit Kingdom in part to celebrate Kim's thirty-first birthday. (Kyodo via AP Images.)

The World's Most Elegant Locker Room

George Washington lives in a life-size oil painting in the East Room of the White House. Right hand extended, palm open, he makes the gesture of an impresario. *Ladies and gentlemen, the 2014 NBA Champion San Antonio Spurs,* he seemed to say as the Spurs filed in on a January day in 2015, filling three rows of risers while some three hundred fans, family, and guests applauded coach Gregg Popovich and his team, including the antiquated Big Three, Tim Duncan, Manu Ginobili, and Tony Parker.

Then, moments later, *Ladies and gentlemen, the President of the United States.* "The Spurs are hard to dislike," Obama said from the podium, despite his own allegiance to the Chicago Bulls.

. . . .

Facing page: Though a devoted Chicago Bulls fan, Obama identified with the workmanlike spirit, advanced age, and silver-and-black colors of the San Antonio Spurs. "They want everybody on the court," said Obama of the 2014 NBA Champions. "They think everybody has worth. . . . And in that sense, they're a great metaphor for what America should be all about." (Pete Souza/The White House.)

"First of all, they're old. . . . There's a reason why the uniform is black and silver. So it makes me feel good to see that folks in advancing years can succeed in a young man's sport."

No briefer had to prep Obama on what to say when basketball teams traipsed through the White House. "I was considering having the Vice-President cover these remarks so I could stay fresh for the State of the Union," he said. "Taking an example from Pop, who sits his stars sometimes." The insider reference elicited roars, as did a nod to Popovich's interlocutory performance art with network sideline reporters: "I want the coach to know that he is not contractually obliged to take questions after the first quarter of my remarks."

Then Obama turned the microphone over to Popovich, who scanned the podium in vain for talking points. "You don't get notes, man," the president said. "Mainly because you just give one-word answers."

By welcoming basketball players to the White House with easy badinage, Obama had a way of turning the place into the world's

most elegant locker room. Nothing captured that atmosphere better than the 2009 Rose Garden visit of the UConn women, which turned into a spontaneous game of P-I-G. "The President is giving his speech," recalled Huskies coach Geno Auriemma, "and he stops and says, 'I think I could take you.' Renee Montgomery says, 'Oh, you think so?' So he says, 'Let's go.' And he just starts walking towards the [South Lawn] court. And Secret Service agents with machine guns start falling out of the trees like acorns. So we go and he takes off his jacket and is shooting that ugly lefthanded shot. Our guys [Montgomery, Maya Moore and Tina Charles] are shooting in dresses and high heels. But give him credit: He made his shots and won fair and square."

Another crop of Huskies women, visiting four years later, photobombed him with bunny ears. Hosts and guests got to be so familiar that Vice President Joe Biden once told Auriemma, "If I had your hair, I'd be President."

During their May 2009 visit, Obama made sure to thank the North

A championship basketball team didn't need a big-time pedigree to earn an invitation from the First Fan. Here the president greets the Tigers of DePauw University, the defending NCAA Division III women's titlists, in the Blue Room in June 2013. (Pete Souza/The White House.)

Carolina Tar Heels for vindicating his NCAA tournament picks. In 2013, LeBron James called Obama "coach" before Obama turned the microphone over to him, saying, "It's your world, man"—after which Obama, once again flaunting his knowledge of the nuances of the NBA, herded the Heat together for a photograph with an admonition: "But we should make it quick before one of these guys starts yelling at Mario"—a reference to Mario Chalmers, a favorite timeout-huddle whipping boy for James and teammate Dwyane Wade.

With light banter usually the order of the day, it was no surprise to see Obama leave a basketball event with a spring in his step. After busting the chops of former Bulls nemeses Bill Laimbeer and Rick Mahorn, the erstwhile Detroit Pistons turned coaches of the WNBA Champion Detroit Shock, the president departed the South Portico with a ball in his hands. He crossover dribbled, went behind his back (a moment captured on the cover of this book), and, finally, flicked the ball over his shoulder toward the Rose Garden.

The White House visit by a championship team has a lengthy history. The first took place in 1925, when Calvin Coolidge, bowing to pressure from locals, belatedly honored the hometown Washington Senators, winners of the 1924 World Series. But the custom of routinely extending invitations across sports didn't kick in until the presidency of Ronald Reagan, the former sportscaster who, while entertaining the 1986 Super Bowl Champion New York Giants, was treated by linebacker Harry Carson to a Gatorade-like bath with a cooler full of popcorn.

In 2006 the Miami Heat presented George W. Bush with a basketball that the president tried to dribble but, it being insufficiently inflated, failed to bounce back. There would be no such sight gags during the Obama administration, which tended assiduously to the details of basketball stagecraft as it ramped up the number of hoop-themed events. That champions of the NBA and WNBA, and NCAA Division I men's and women's tournaments, would be invited went without saying. But Obama welcomed basketball teams and figures from farther afield, including the 2013 NCAA Division III Champion DePauw women, the surviving members of Loyola's 1963 NCAA Champions, and such Presidential Medal of Freedom recipients as Bill Russell and Pat Summitt. Teams with connections to the First Lady's brother, Oregon State coach Craig Robinson, also passed through, including several editions

Storage areas in the White House gift unit filled up with a disproportionate number of basketball-related presents. Virtually every team to visit, such as Duke's 2010 NCAA Champions shown here, brought the gift of a personalized jersey. (Pete Souza/ The White House.)

After winning their second straight NBA title, the Los Angeles Lakers were grateful for a variation on the usual White House visit when they passed through Washington in December 2010. Here coach Phil Jackson and the president join kids at a local Boys and Girls Club to prepare care packages for troops overseas. (Pete Souza/The White House.)

over the years, members of the 2010 NBA Champion Los Angeles Lakers such as Kobe Bryant and coach Phil Jackson were happy to mix things up. (Of going to the White House, said Jackson, "The thrill is gone, as B. B. King said.") So Obama honored those Lakers at a Boys and Girls Club in Southeast D.C., where several dozen kids served as the audience and, afterward, everyone—kids, Lakers, and POTUS alike—assembled care packages for soldiers and toiletries kits for the homeless.

The Spurs spent the morning of their 2015 visit looking in on wounded veterans at Walter Reed National Military Medical Center and Fort Belvoir. Just before the ceremony honoring them, White House spokesman Josh Earnest had

of Robinson's Beavers, as well as the Princeton women's team on which Craig's daughter Leslie played. "What's fun is when the women basketball players come in, because they're all gorgeous and they're all six-foot-five and wearing high heels," Obama said. "And so they're walking through the West Wing and everybody is wondering what the heck is going on."

Obama had a close connection to the Rooney family, owners of the Pittsburgh Steelers, and noted how the Steelers, when they visited the White House after their 2009 Super Bowl title, carved out time to visit military families. After that, the administration urged visiting teams to fold a community-service project into their trips. Jaded by multiple visits

The surviving members of Loyola's 1963 NCAA Champions visit the Oval Office, where captain Jerry Harkness presents Obama with framed mementos of "the Game of Change." The Ramblers' four black starters met all-white Mississippi State in the NCAA tournament after the Bulldogs, sneaking out of the state under cover of darkness, defied a court order not to play an integrated team. (Pete Souza/The White House.)

been spit-roasted at the daily press briefing for the administration's failure to send a high-ranking official to Paris for the previous day's rally against the *Charlie Hebdo* shootings. It had been a mistake, Earnest admitted. Obama made no mention of the controversy, but there was an implied solidarity in that East Room tableau. Parker, a French citizen, stood by the president's right shoulder. Countryman Boris Diaw loomed over his left. "This is an international team," Obama said. "It's the U.N. of basketball teams. And it shows the way that this wonderful sport has become an international sport."

The Spurs weren't the Bulls, but they were an Obamaesque crew in many ways. The president touched on several in his praise for them: their devotion to the commons, as expressed by their artful passing ("the beautiful game . . . basketball the way it should be played," he said); their even temper ("boring"—and he meant it as a compliment); their workaday focus on the long-range goal, not unlike the man known as No Drama Obama. "He knows who we are," Popovich said afterward. "It was very flattering to hear him say those things. We're not big camera people or beat-our-chest kind of people. . . . We say, 'Do your job and go home.'"

After namechecking Parker and Diaw, as well as Ginobili of Argentina, Tiago Splitter of Brazil, Patty Mills of Australia, Marco Belinelli of Italy, and Becky Hammon, the former WNBA star who was in her first season as a Spurs assistant coach, Obama said, "What the Spurs do—they find ways to put together the best team, whether that means going to Australia or Italy or the WNBA. They want everybody on the court. They think everybody has worth. They find folks who didn't have a chance someplace else and suddenly they figure out a way to make them shine as part of a team. And in that sense, they're a great metaphor for what America should be all about."∎

. . . .

Facing page: Leaving the South Portico, the president waves good-bye to the freshly crowned 2009 NCAA Champion North Carolina Tar Heels. A year earlier Obama had scrimmaged with the team on the campaign trail, and in his first tournament bracket as president, he successfully predicted their title. (Pete Souza/The White House.)

The Loyal Opposition

With adherents who skew young, urban, and ethnic, and a scuffling untidiness to its nature, basketball shares many of the characteristics of the modern Democratic Party. But even as Obama and his team put their stamp on pebblegrain Washington, the sport found followers among Republicans too.

Jeff Flake of Arizona brought a sweet baseline jumper to regular games in the Senate gym. Rep. Zach Wamp of Tennessee was known for his feisty defense. But it was John Thune, a 6'4" senator from South Dakota, who was mentioned most often as the finest player the Republicans had. "Look, Barack Obama's good, but

Shown here are two of the best ballplayers in GOP Washington, Arizona senator Jeff Flake (*foreground*), then in the House, and South Dakota senator John Thune, in transition during Team Congress's 39–38 defeat of Team K Street in the 2010 Hoops for Hope Congressional All-Star Classic at George Washington University.

(Photo by Tom Williams/*Roll Call*/Getty Images.)

he's definitely not the best basketball player in the Senate," one GOP senator said of the then president-elect. "Not by a long shot. John Thune is the best basketball player in the Senate. Bar none."

Some of the president's most implacable opponents could point to hoop backgrounds. Of Sarah (Barracuda) Palin, co-captain and point guard on Wasilla High's 1982 Alaska state championship team, Obama during the 2008 campaign said, "It looks like she's got some game." In 2013–2014 Wichita State completed a 31–0 regular season, its greatest ever, while playing in Charles Koch Arena, named after and funded by the elder of the billionaire Koch brothers. For nearly a half-century Charles's younger brother and comrade in right-wing PAC money, David, graced the MIT record book as the school's top single-game scorer; in November 2008, after breaking Koch's record of 41 by springing for 43 points, Engineers senior Jimmy Bartolotta said that the old mark would likely still stand if David Koch had played with the three-point shot.

With the game so closely identified

with Obama, basketball became fodder in Republican hands from the moment he announced a run for the White House. As the Democrats' narrative held that their guy played with smarts and finesse, Gov. Arnold Schwarzenegger (R-Calif.) called out the candidate's "scrawny little arms." Republican strategist Karl Rove described Obama's condescending remark to his main rival during a 2008 primary debate—"You're likeable enough, Hillary"—as "trash talking . . . an unattractive carryover from his days playing pickup basketball at Harvard." It was a Rove two-fer, a way to paint Obama as elitist and thug at the same time. After Obama sank a three-pointer during a visit to a military base in Kuwait, the McCain campaign used the footage in an attack ad, insinuating that the candidate was an insubstantial celebrity with no respect for the troops. In the judgment of *New York* magazine's John Heilemann, the spot's racial subtext drew a portrait of "Allen Iverson with a Harvard Law degree."

Once Obama assumed office, the president's race weaponized suggestions that basketball was a sign of lassitude or laziness. GOP presidential candidate Newt Gingrich's comments on Fox News in 2012 included enough dog whistles to wake up a kennel: "He's a false President. He's a guy that doesn't do the President's job. . . . I'm assuming that there's some rhythm to Barack Obama that the rest of us don't understand. Whether he needs large amounts of rest, whether he needs to go play basketball for a while or watch ESPN, I mean, I don't quite know what his rhythm is."

Yet even as the GOP's most aggressive voices tried to turn the game into a mark of the alien, basketball found its way into intramural Republican politics too. In 2014 former Purdue star Curt Clawson won a three-way primary in Florida's Nineteenth Congressional District thanks in part to a TV spot called "The Outsider," in which he challenged Obama to a three-point shooting contest. "I hope he'll have a look at the video," Clawson told a Tampa TV reporter, "man up a little bit, send me an invitation, and let's settle it on the court." David Brat, the economics professor and Tea Party

Two of the billionaire Koch brothers, David (*left*) and William, played together at MIT. David graduated in 1962 with the school's single-game scoring record, which stood for nearly a half-century. (Courtesy of MIT Museum.)

favorite who took out House Majority Leader Eric Cantor (R-Va.) during the same primary season, was a noon-hoop regular on the Randolph-Macon University campus, often playing with the Democrat he would beat in the general election, sociology professor Jack Trammell. Mississippi Republican Chris McDaniel might have addressed a neo-Confederate group, but the unsuccessful 2014 GOP Senate candidate couldn't possibly harbor retrograde racial attitudes, argued an editorial in his hometown newspaper, the *Laurel* (Mississippi) *Leader-Call,* because "McDaniel was a basketball standout at South Jones [High School] and Jones County Junior College. At the risk of stereotyping, what color do you think his buddies were on those teams?"

When Rep. John Shimkus (R-Ill.) was invited to play at the White House in 2009, he pronounced himself "grateful for the invitation" and "[looked] forward to a competitive game," which afterward he called "enjoyable."

Given that Shimkus had walked out of the president's address to Congress on health care only a month earlier, basketball seemed to have played some conciliatory role.■

The Inevitability of Golf

"If I had my way," H. L. Mencken wrote in 1943, "no man guilty of golf would be eligible to any office of trust under the United States." The Bard of Baltimore did not get his way, for the game has incriminated almost every president since, with only Harry Truman and Jimmy Carter escaping its snares. Obama's innocence barely lasted until the cherry trees bloomed during his first spring in office, when he began to play almost every weekend he was in town. "You cannot play if you permit yourself to think of anything else," William Howard Taft once said of the game—and that's where much of golf's appeal to a chief executive lies.

Even if the game almost always claims a president, how exactly did it get its hooks in Obama? Precisely

. . . .

The deeper he advanced into his presidency, the more Obama appreciated the refuge of a round of golf. Here he winds up for a tee shot at the Kaneohe Klipper Marine Golf Course on Oahu during a December 2010 holiday visit to Hawaii, the state of his birth. (Pete Souza/The White House.)

Power, Forward

107

because Obama was so serious about basketball—after assuming the presidency he played hoop mostly indoors, with others who refused to take the game lightly—golf supplied welcome changes of pace and place. It was, Obama said in 2009, "the closest thing to being outside of the bubble . . . [and] the only time I'm outside for any sizable stretch of time." And it offered a semblance of privacy: "There are a whole bunch of Secret Service guys, but they're sort of in the woods."

Conversely, when Obama laced up his basketball shoes, said Sen. Robert Casey (D-Pa.), an occasional participant in presidential pickup games, "he plays hard. It may not be relaxing enough."

Arthur Jackson, a regular in the president's Saturday morning full-court run, believed he could pinpoint the day basketball began to yield to golf. It was that morning in November 2010 when Obama took an elbow to the mouth at Fort McNair and needed twelve stitches to close a cut lip. In the moments after the incident, Jackson said, "you could see in his face everything he had to do in the world.

The game had been an escape, and suddenly he had to concern himself with this hole in his mouth."

Obama could play basketball at one speed only. "You play in these competitive games, with people talking a lot of trash and bragging rights on the line until next time, and the level of intensity is through the roof," said former personal aide Reggie Love, who played in virtually every game his boss did until he left the White House before the 2012 campaign. "He's a person who bleeds it. It's not a hobby thing."

And golf was indeed a hobby— even if by all accounts Obama played earnestly, stroking out every hole and swearing off mulligans. "It's a game that I keep on thinking I should be good at," said Obama, a 17 handicapper, in 2009, voicing something often heard from basketball players who take up the game (ball, receptacle—what could go wrong?). "And somehow the ball goes this way and that way and never goes straight."

In August 2014 Obama played what he called the best round of his life, coming within a fifteen-

foot putt of breaking 80. The eight rounds he played in eleven days that month, during a vacation on Martha's Vineyard, wouldn't have raised an eyebrow if not for the circumstances of one of those outings. On August 20 the president expressed horror at the execution of James Foley, an American journalist kidnapped and held by ISIS in Syria. To the press he described himself as "heartbroken," and he looked the part. That he then went off to play a round with Alonzo Mourning and Ray Allen recalled George W. Bush's 2002 tee-box segue from a denunciation of terrorism to "Now, watch this drive!" Obama later said he regretted doing so. But by then the D.C. pundit class, already faulting him for failing to schmooze the town's power brokers, had further noted that Obama usually played with junior aides and friends, not insiders he could cajole or political opponents with whom he might build bridges.

A right-wing website called ObamaGolfCounter.com tried to turn Obama's golfing into an issue, toting up 208 outings as of February 2015. Yet the presidential record of Dwight Eisenhower remained far out of reach. The master of the thirty-six-hole workweek played nearly eight hundred rounds over eight years, and found time for another couple hundred or so sessions of putting or chipping, mostly on the green with a small sand trap that the U.S. Golf Association installed for him outside the Oval Office in 1954. In the meantime Obama found encouragement from less ideological quarters. "Basketball may have more street cred, but golf will make Mr. Obama a better president," wrote *The Economist* in an editorial. "Basketball requires instant reactions in the heat of the moment. Golf requires patience and strategy, calmly executed."

But others argued to the contrary. Golf, they said, made Obama seem like any other president. Eight months into Obama's first term, *Sanford* (North Carolina) *Herald* columnist Alex Podlogar pleaded with him to get back on the court. "Let me put it in language you might be better able to understand, Mr. President," he wrote. "Basketball? Yes, you can. Golf? No, you can't." In the aftermath of Democratic losses in the 2014 midterms, Edward Alden, a fellow at the Council on Foreign Relations who enjoyed both sports, issued much the same appeal. A president boxed in by a hostile Congress and suffering from an approval rating in the forties, Alden argued, needed less of the Zen detachment that makes for a good golfer and more of the in-the-mix feistiness that hoop demands.

In fact, how a chief executive spends his rare free time is a jealously guarded presidential prerogative for good reason. That choice, like so many others, is for POTUS alone to make.■

The president shakes hands with LeBron James in a Verizon Center locker room at halftime during the U.S. men's national team's tune-up against Brazil in advance of the 2012 London Olympics. *At left:* Michelle Obama hugs James's teammate Deron Williams. (Pete Souza/The White House.)

THE GAME IN THE
AGE OF OBAMA

In late 2008, as Barack Obama prepared to move into the White House, pro basketball was just beginning to stir from a prolonged funk. The NBA had spent a dozen years searching for names to replace Larry Bird, Magic Johnson, and Michael Jordan on its marquees, and for ways to move past a series of stains on its image. In 1997 Latrell Sprewell choked his coach, P. J. Carlesimo, during a Golden State Warriors practice. In 2003 prosecutors in Colorado pressed a sexual-assault case against Los Angeles Lakers star Kobe Bryant, who would see the charge dropped only after more than a year of tawdry news coverage. No sooner had the Bryant affair left the headlines than "the Malice at the Palace" sent a shudder through the league. During a game at the Palace of Auburn Hills, Michigan, in November 2004, the Indiana Pacers' Ron Artest waded into the stands to attack an abusive Detroit Pistons fan, touching off a brawl

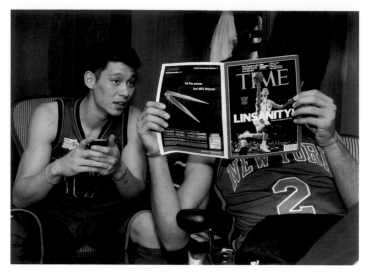

In the space of a few weeks in 2012, Jeremy Lin took the New York Knicks and the NBA, as well as millions of Asian Americans who identified with him, on a ride through the looking glass. (Copyright © 2012 NBA Entertainment. Photo by Kent Smith/NBAE/Getty Images.)

that led to almost $12 million in fines and disciplinary action against nine players.

Well before the lengthy stewardship of commissioner David Stern, the NBA stood as the most progressive of the major pro sports leagues. By the sixties, even as some college coaches still observed the informal rule that you played "one [black player] at home, two on the road and three when you're behind," Boston Celtics coach and general manager Red Auerbach was already winning NBA titles with African American talent. Decades later Stern, an old-line civil rights and labor lawyer, would preside over the league's consistent collection of high marks in the annual

racial and gender report cards issued by the University of Central Florida's Institute for Diversity and Ethics in Sport, and would earn praise for fining Bryant $100,000 and Joakim Noah of the Chicago Bulls $50,000 for using anti-gay slurs during games.

Yet Stern's response to those post-Jordan public relations challenges alienated many players. He imposed a dress code, mandating fines for being photographed or filmed in baggy pants or gold chains. He huddled with GOP-connected consultant Matthew Dowd for advice on how to enhance the league's appeal to culturally conservative fans. Players took particular offense when *Hoop,* the NBA's official magazine, airbrushed tattoos out of a photo of Philadelphia 76ers guard Allen Iverson, the league's most iconoclastic star.

Enter Obama, who became a figure over whom labor and management could broadly agree. Stern openly supported his election, and players throughout the league gave his campaign their money and endorsements (see "Players' Choice," page 51). "This is a huge deal for our country and the world," Stern said after the votes were counted in November 2008. "Forget about our brand as it relates to this. The question is, what can we do to help him?"

To the players, Obama was an African American president who loved, and still played, ball. NBA executives recognized his youth and international appeal, as well as his popularity with the core of the league's fan base. Basketball was a cultural and generational marker, and Obama could claim credibility on both scores. The president exchanged daps with the First Lady and personal aide Reggie Love, while around the country even members of all-white high school teams sprinted over to referees during pregame introductions to do the same—all of which exposed the Fox News commentator who called the gesture "a terrorist fist jab" as pitiably out of touch. "The way we saw it," said Adam Silver, then Stern's deputy, "a vote for Obama was a vote for basketball."

Indeed, in the aftermath of the 2008 election, chickens found their way into a multitude of hoop pots. While Obama served as steward of the country of basketball's birth, the pro game flourished in new markets as diverse as red-state Oklahoma City and left-leaning Brooklyn. It rode its own ethnic-themed story, the rise of Jeremy Lin, as unlikely as Obama's ascent to the Oval Office. With their far-flung backgrounds and cohesive style, the 2014 NBA Champion San Antonio Spurs enshrined as virtues the very exoticism and communitarianism that Obama's political opponents tried to assign to him as vices. Even the tactical vogue that had marked basketball since the late 2000s—the emergence of dribble-drive offenses at every level of the game—mirrored the beat-'em-off-the-bounce style Obama himself preferred to play.

Meanwhile a cavalcade of firsts made its way through the sport. An NBA free agent named Jason Collins, eventually signed by the Brooklyn Nets, became the first active American male athlete in a professional team sport to come out. Women found places throughout pro basketball, including Becky Hammon, an assistant on the Spurs' bench; executives such as the Lakers' Jeanie Buss, the Los Angeles Clippers' Gillian Zucker, and the New Orleans Pelicans' Rita Benson Leblanc; and Michele Roberts, who took over the NBA Players Association in 2014. And front-office leadership was vested with everyone from Burmese-born Rich Cho of the Charlotte Hornets, to Nigerian-born Masai Ujiri of the Denver Nuggets and Toronto Raptors, to someone who checked boxes in two categories, Nets president Irina Pavlova, a Russian-born woman.

In the most striking development, more and more players began to focus on the world beyond the baselines and see it by the light of politics. By wearing jerseys reading "Los Suns" on Cinco de Mayo in 2010, the Phoenix Suns protested anti-immigrant legislation in Arizona. The Miami Heat posed in hoodies to protest the killing of Florida teenager Trayvon Martin, slain by a vigilante in Febru-

With sublime ball movement and a polyglot pedigree, the San Antonio Spurs set a high basketball bar during the Age of Obama and captured the era well. *From left:* Tony Parker, Tim Duncan, and Manu Ginobili celebrate after the Spurs breezed past the Miami Heat to win the 2014 NBA title. (Brendan Maloney—*USA TODAY* Sports.)

Steve Nash and the Phoenix Suns honored Arizona's Latinos—
and took a public shot at the state's controversial anti-immigrant
legislation—by wearing "Los Suns" uniforms on Cinco de Mayo in
2010. (Mark J. Rebilas—*USA TODAY* Sports.)

part of our democracy," Obama said after the Suns, including owner Robert Sarver, made their pro-immigrant statement. "I think it's terrific that the Suns, who obviously feel very strongly about their community, recognize that a big part of their community felt threatened by this new law.

"That people are engaged in the big issues of the day I think is a positive thing and I don't think either players or franchises need to always steer away from controversy."

Presidents are trained to ignore questions shouted as they leave a press conference podium. But in April 2013 a query about Jason Collins caused Obama to pivot and return to the microphone, where he went on for several minutes about Collins's ability to say, "This is who I am, I'm proud of it, I'm still a great competitor, I'm still seven-foot tall and can bang with Shaq and deliver a hard foul . . . and for I think a lot of young people out there who are gay or lesbian who are struggling with these issues, to see a role model like that who is unafraid, I think it's a great thing."

Unbeknownst to Obama, a redshirt sophomore guard at the University of Massachusetts was indeed "struggling with these issues." A year later, after he too came out, Derrick Gordon credited the public support Collins received with helping to ease his decision, and in November 2014 Gordon became the first man to play in a Division I basketball game while openly gay. "Everything leads to the NBA for me, and I didn't want my dreams to be shattered because of my sexuality," Gordon said. "So when I saw him come out, that inspired me."

Active players curious about what a publicly engaged retirement might look like had a Hall of Fame example in Magic Johnson. After being diagnosed as HIV positive in

ary 2012 when Martin ventured out into a Sanford, Florida, street while wearing a hooded sweatshirt at halftime of the NBA All-Star Game. In 2011 the Milwaukee Bucks signaled support for public-sector employees in Wisconsin who had been stripped of their collective-bargaining rights. "Just because somebody's a sports figure who has got a sports team doesn't mean you're not part of the community or

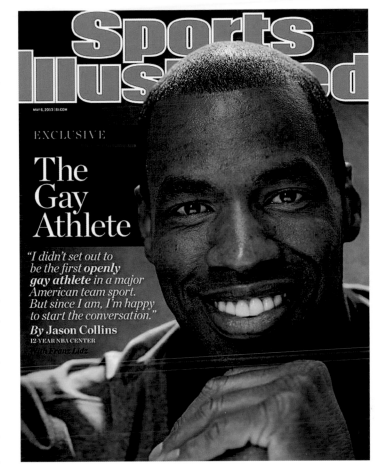

1991, Johnson took advantage of his status as a long-term nonprogressor, devoting himself to doing well by doing good. His $1 billion conglomerate, Magic Johnson Enterprises, pumped capital into ethnically diverse urban areas, delivering leisure-time options that gentrified, whiter neighborhoods took for granted—cinemas, coffeehouses, and pro sports teams, like the WNBA's Los Angeles Sparks. Other MJE interests had an explicitly progressive mission: a chain of academies where a high-school dropout could pick up a G.E.D., a health-care provider that specialized in serving the HIV-positive population, an institutional caterer that supplied nutritious options to schools in inner-city food deserts. In the words of Stern, "Magic has set the standard for post-career social responsibility."

Johnson's announcement that he was HIV positive, Obama said at a November 2013 Democratic fundraiser held at the former Laker's Beverly Hills home, prompted "the country and the world to think in an entirely new way that ends up changing the face of this country and our attitudes with the kind of grace and courage that only true leaders can display.

"Magic has become our prime example of somebody who was blessed with incredible fame and fortune from a sports career and understood his next step is to build institutions and businesses, and employ people."

As ballplayers were drawn to influence events around them, events sometimes exerted a pull on those connected to the game, with players and coaches raising a hand or a voice as if summoned by the moment. Magic's old Showtime teammate, Kareem Abdul-Jabbar, became a prominent public voice, using regular online columns and TV appearances to weigh in on such topics as Islamophobia

Magic Johnson, shown here in 2013 giving POTUS a tour of the trophy room in his Beverly Hills home, "understood his next step is to build institutions and businesses, and employ people," said Obama. (Pete Souza/The White House.)

and the urban underclass. College coaches Jim Boeheim of Syracuse and Pat Kelsey of Wofford implored Obama and others in Washington to pass legislation in the wake of the 2012 Newtown school shootings. Former NBA All-Star floor leaders Kevin Johnson and Dave Bing ran for mayor as reform candidates in Sacramento and Detroit, respectively, where voters entrusted each with the task of leading

their city back from fiscal distress. When a Navy helicopter crashed during the raid on Osama bin Laden's compound in Pakistan in May 2011, members of Seal Team Six reverted to schoolyard instincts to turn the operation into a success. "Shoot, move and communicate," said Matt Bissonnette, a commando who wrote an account of the operation under the pen name Mark Owen. "We all know how to shoot. We all know how to move efficiently and tactically. And we can communicate clearly. So when something goes sideways, we're able to play the pickup basketball and just kind of read off each other."

It's not clear that Michael Jordan actually said "Republicans buy sneakers, too." The provenance of that comment, long attributed to him, is vague. Jordan might have said something like it to a friend, or some third party might have delivered the remark as commentary on Jordan's studiously apolitical persona. But there's no doubt about the context of the sentiment, apocryphal though the statement might be. The words explained why Jordan declined to endorse Harvey Gantt, the African American mayor of Charlotte, in a 1990 North Carolina Senate campaign against the race-baiting incumbent Jesse Helms. And they captured the Zeitgeist of the eighties and nineties, a time of *Jerry Maguire* and "Show me the money!" and the athlete-agent mind meld—"an era characterized not by raised fists, but by open palms," as *The Observer* of London put it. Why alienate a potential fan and, worse, leave money on the table?

By the time Obama was elected, much of the Millennial generation had become eligible to vote. And Millennials, a cohort predisposed to idealism and speaking one's mind, helped change the political profile of the NBA's locker rooms. In April 2014, LeBron James and his Miami Heat teammates were among the players to wear warm-up shirts inside-out in solidarity with Los Angeles Clippers angry with their owner, Donald Sterling. In 2009 Sterling, a southern California slumlord, had paid a $2.73 million fine to settle housing discrimination charges even before his racist comments surfaced on a leaked tape.

The killing of Trayvon Martin in 2012 also heightened the sensitivity of NBA players to the world around them. "These kids come from the same neighborhoods we walked—or worse," said Greg Monroe of the Detroit Pistons after he and others jumped into a national discussion of racial profiling. "When we get pulled over, there's no special millionaire cops." Beyond the arena and TV cameras, an NBA player was likely to be seen as just another young black male, even if he happened to be paid extravagantly to play basketball.

It was one of the most reticent of the NBA's players, Derrick Rose of the Chicago Bulls, who first wore an "I Can't Breathe" warm-up shirt after a grand jury declined to bring charges against the New York City policeman responsible for the choking death of suspect Eric Garner. Rose was moved to do so after he and two childhood friends, from a window of his downtown Chicago apartment, watched a

. . . .

Inspired by protesters on the street below his Chicago apartment, as well as by memories of his own upbringing on the city's South Side, Derrick Rose of the Bulls pulled on this shirt and set a trend in the aftermath of Eric Garner's death. (Dennis Wierzbicki—*USA TODAY* Sports.)

demonstration on the street below. Regardless of his own feelings about the issue Rose raised, NBA commissioner Adam Silver frowned on the gesture, for he believed the 94-by-50-foot dimensions of an NBA floor should be a politics-free zone. But he understood why Rose chose the United Center, which sits on Chicago's South Side, as his

forum. "Our arenas are in some ways the modern-day equivalents of town halls in major urban areas," Silver said. "And I think our players recognize that."

Two days later, at a game between the Cleveland Cavaliers and the Brooklyn Nets, James joined teammate Kyrie Irving and the Nets' Kevin Garnett, Deron Williams, Alan Anderson, and Jarrett Jack in wearing the shirts. Outside Brooklyn's Barclays Center demonstrators staged a "die-in," while inside Prince Harry and his wife, Kate Middleton, sat courtside with Beyoncé and her husband, Jay-Z, who had helped arrange for delivery of the shirts to the players. "Obviously we're not on the frontline of this movement," Garnett said. "But I think it's important to give to these communities and support these communities."

Meanwhile basketball players had already protested the shooting death of Michael Brown in Ferguson, Missouri, four months earlier. Before a game against Fontbonne College in Clayton, Missouri, near the site of the incident, Ariyana Smith, a player for the women's team at Division III Knox College, made the "hands up, don't shoot" gesture during the playing of the national anthem. Then Smith delayed tipoff by lying on the floor for four and a half minutes, the duration of her protest calculated to reflect the four and a half hours that Brown's corpse had lain uncollected on Ferguson's Canfield Drive. Once her protest concluded, Smith left the building with a fist in the air. She was suspended from the team but quickly reinstated by officials at Knox, a school founded by figures in the anti-slavery movement.

The demonstrations enticed people far beyond the world of sports to take notice. "LeBron is in your living room," observed political blogger Josh Marshall. "And he's awesome. But we don't go there. But he is going there. And that just upsets the sports and race apple cart—by bringing big divisions in American society right into the open."

It's impossible to determine how much Obama figured in the politicization of the NBA's labor force. But his candidacy, presidency, and identification with the game had caught the attention of virtually everyone in the sport. One player, Jason Collins's twin brother and Utah Jazz center Jarron Collins, placed his rise in context: "It's the Jay-Z line. Rosa sat, so Martin could walk, so Obama could run, so we all could fly."

Once politically attuned, and with prominent platforms and social media tools at their disposal, players hardly needed marching orders from the White House. Simply by noticing and endorsing their engagement, the president amplified it. "We went through a long stretch there where [with] well-paid athletes the notion was, just be quiet and get your endorsements and don't make waves," Obama said. "LeBron is an example of a young man who has, in his own way and in a respectful way, tried to say, 'I'm part of this society too' and focus attention. I'd like to see more athletes do that. Not just around [the Eric Garner] issue, but around a range of issues."

And if supporting candidates and causes compromised a player's ability to land endorsement deals, the Detroit Pistons' Chauncey Billups spoke for a generation. "Like," he said, "I give a shit."

While Jordan had supported Obama's 2004 Illinois Senate campaign, in 2008 he hung back, even as another former Tar Heel, Vince Carter, publicly threw his support to Obama, as did Grant Hill, a graduate of rival Duke. It wasn't until the president's reelection campaign, in August 2012, that Jordan made his presidential coming-out. He joined Stern to co-host the Obama Classic, a $20,000-a-plate fundraiser at Manhattan's Lincoln Center that featured several dozen active and former NBA and WNBA players. The event affirmed that, on this score, labor and management stood united.

Though he didn't take a public position during the 2008 campaign, Jordan had been watching. And apparently some things were worth more than a sneaker sale. On the night Obama was first elected, Jordan confessed, "I was cryin' like a damn baby."

If Barack Obama were bald and Jewish, it would be hard to distinguish him from Adam Silver. David Stern's successor as NBA commissioner was Obama's age. He was also lean and literary, with stints both in D.C. politics and at the University of Chicago Law School on his résumé. As a law student Silver had even volunteered in Obama's old community organizing haunts on the South Side, taking on employment and housing discrimination cases at a legal aid clinic.

In April 2014, not two weeks after his first Board of Governors meeting, Silver banned for life the Clippers' Sterling, one of the owners he answered to. "There's a commercial side to our players, but there's also a political side, and I was able to do what I did, and do it swiftly, because I wasn't acting in a vacuum," said Silver, referring to the engagement of others, including Clippers star and NBA

With swift disciplinary action against misbehaving owners and players alike, Adam Silver won wide respect soon after replacing David Stern as NBA commissioner in February 2014. (Kim Klement—*USA TODAY Sports*.)

Players Association president Chris Paul. "I was acting sort of on behalf of the NBA family, as a partner with our teams and partner with our players."

Soon thereafter an audiotape emerged of Atlanta Hawks general manager Danny Ferry denigrating the African heritage of Sudanese forward Luol Deng, and further investigation turned up e-mails implicating controlling owner Bruce Levenson in assertions that the team's African American fans "scared away the whites" and the Kiss Cam at Philips Arena was "too black." Here Silver hardly had to respond; Ferry asked to take an indefinite leave, and Levenson agreed to step aside until the Hawks could be sold. Antisocial behavior in the NBA could no longer be blamed on some incorrigible hip-hop generation. It had become lodged in the league's executive suites. Silver made clear that it wouldn't be tolerated anywhere.

In October 2014 the NBA concluded its first TV rights negotiation under Silver's leadership—a deal with Disney and Time Warner that almost tripled the value of the existing contract, from $940 million to $2.66 billion a year. The league could command those terms for a simple reason: In an age of web streaming and time shifting—as more and more Americans consumed entertainment on their own schedules, binge-watching a Netflix series or Slingboxing a primetime episode on a whim—advertisers loved that live televised sports couldn't be watched on demand or stripped of commercials. Because they induced a mass audience to sit down together as one, sports had an outsized impact on the culture. And as action unspooled, viewers interacted with one another on Twitter and by text message in real time, engaging in a vigorously social "second-screen experience." With more women tuning in than ever before, sports audiences replicated that fifties focus-group family once gathered around the Philco in the tract-home den. Kenny Smith and Charles Barkley of TNT's *Inside the NBA* had become stars of a modern *Smothers Brothers Comedy Hour.*

If sports came to serve as a staging ground for national conversations about not just police reform and gay rights but also concussions, domestic violence, child abuse, and racial sensitivity, it was because American society featured a vanishing number of public squares in which discussion of any kind could take place. To be sure, the 186 percent spike in NBA rights fees would show up in advertisers' pass-along costs and cable carriage fees. But those surcharges were paying for shared thrills, reality TV that couldn't be manipulated, and community—in short, one of the last throwback, common experiences in the culture. And if the marketplace determined that the extra cost was worth it, here again labor and management could stand shoulder to shoulder. The windfall would accrue to the handsome benefit of, to use a favorite locution of Stern and Silver alike, "the NBA and its players."

If a public consensus had formed on any issue beyond the NBA during the Age of Obama, it was that college athletes had no friend in the NCAA. Critics of the college sports status quo fell into two camps. Revolutionaries, such as sneaker impresario Sonny Vaccaro, *New York Times* columnist Joe Nocera, and civil rights historian and Bill Russell biographer Taylor Branch, wanted to end the sham of amateurism and pay revenue-generating football and men's basketball players a market wage. Reformers, such as members of the Knight Commission and the professors and administrators affiliated with the Drake Group, didn't want to create two classes of athletes, much less decouple athletics from academics, but instead sought to bring the sports beast to heel with carrots and sticks. Given the administration's moderate policy inclinations, Obama and his secretary of education, Arne Duncan, unsurprisingly sided with the reformers. "I do think that recognizing that the majority of these student-athletes are not going to end up playing professional ball—this isn't just a farm system for the NBA or the NFL—means that the universities have more responsibilities than right now they're showing," Obama said in March 2015.

"Arne and the President agree," added Reggie Love, who knew their thinking well. "The incentive structure in college sports is warped."

Under its late president Myles Brand, the NCAA had taken steps in the reformers' direction, barring from postseason play any school that failed to achieve a satisfactory academic progress rate, or APR, the metric that measured the progress a team's athletes made toward a degree. But the minimum was set far too low to be much of a deterrent. At the 2010 NCAA Convention in Atlanta, Duncan delivered an impassioned call to raise the graduation-rate requirement. "I did not get a standing ovation that week," noted Duncan, who had been a basketball co-captain at Harvard. "But we pushed very hard for [a higher minimum] and actually made it happen. We took some heat, but I'm proud of that."

In 2013 the University of Connecticut became the first major school to sit out an NCAA tournament for APR deficiencies in its men's basketball program. "A team that has 13 or 15% of its African American guys graduate—you're just using those guys," Duncan said that year. "We want to make sure that those teams that get rewarded by going to the tournament do the right thing by getting it done in the classroom first. . . . Everyone wants to go to a Division I

school because they want to play in the tournament. That's the payoff. [But] if [a school's] not eligible, [a player's] going to go someplace else. You have to change behavior."

In December 2014, Duncan and a representative of the White House met with congressmen and members of the Drake Group to discuss ways the administration might push college sports reform even further along, including steps to address such issues as academic fraud, scholarship security, and escalating coaches' salaries. One option was to form a presidential commission, modeled on Gerald Ford's 1975 initiative that led to the eclipse of the Amateur Athletic Union by the U.S. Olympic Committee. "The secretary indicated that the President is very interested in the issue," said Rep. Jim Moran (D-Va.), the outgoing congressman who led the delegation. A month later two Democrats, Bobby Rush (D-Ill.) and Bobby Scott (D-Va.), and two Republicans, Joe Barton (R-Tex.) and Charlie Dent (R-Pa.), introduced into the 114th Congress H.R. 275, a bill that would establish a presidential commission "to identify and examine issues of national concern related to the conduct of intercollegiate athletics and to make recommendations for the resolution of such issues."

If the ESPN-obsessed bracketologist in the Oval Office were to take up the cause of reform, it would constitute an ironic turn in one respect. In 2014 Connecticut defeated Kentucky for the NCAA title in the Huskies' first season following that ban for failing to meet APR standards. In the flush of victory, UConn guard Shabazz Napier defiantly told the nation, "Let me get your attention! Ladies and gentlemen, you're looking at the hungry Huskies! This is what happens when you ban us!"

A politicized Shabazz Napier uses a CBS microphone to call out the NCAA, whose 2014 title he and his UConn teammates have just won. The Obama administration pressured the NCAA to raise the very graduation-rate standards that had sidelined the Huskies the previous season. (Matthew Emmons—*USA TODAY* Sports.)

It wasn't the NCAA's idea of "one shining moment," even if it was singular and impossible to miss. To watch Napier that night, alongside the frozen face of his interviewer, Jim Nantz of CBS, was to see a member of the Obama generation empowered by the political consciousness trickling down through the game. Yet the president and his secretary of education stood squarely with the spirit and intent of the modest academic expectations that had sidelined Napier and his school the previous season. If anything, they wanted to see even stronger incentives and penalties. "I still think the bar should be raised higher," said Duncan. "People thought the NCAA would never change. And they did. And UConn, the poster child for not graduating players, is now graduating them. The battle's not won, but that was real progress."

It wasn't clear how much political capital the president would choose to invest in the college sports reform movement, especially with his time in office winding down. The work mandated by H.R. 275 might be left to another Congress and president. But the clash between athletics and academics, and the administration's instinct to reconcile the two, had an emblematic quality. Here again was a search for equilibrium, a tension between counterposed forces, that was of a piece with the basketball man in the White House—one more manifestation of a characteristic shared by the game and Barack Obama alike.

Shooting the First Shooter

During his more than forty years as a photojournalist, Pete Souza once rode horseback through the snow-covered Hindu Kush to cover the fall of Kabul following the September 11 attacks. But his most fateful assignment came in 2005 when, as a staffer in the Washington bureau of the *Chicago Tribune,* he documented the arrival in D.C. of a young senator from Illinois. The two developed a rapport during the course of that project, which resulted in a 2008 book, *The Rise of Barack Obama.* And when Obama ascended to the presidency, Souza's previous work as official White House photographer under President Reagan helped him get the nod for the same job in the new administration.

Back in the seventies, getting his start at a couple of small newspapers in Kansas, Souza shot sports often. "It's not easy," he said. "You've got to do it all the time to stay sharp." A move to news and politics caused Souza's sports chops to deteriorate. But to document the presidency of

Official White House photographer Pete Souza and the president dash across the tarmac from Air Force One during a 2010 visit to Indiana. (AP Photo/J. Scott Applewhite.)

The Game in the Age of Obama

123

a man who played basketball often, he had to scrape off the rust. One aspect of his mandate eased the transition: "I'm essentially zooming in on one guy. Whereas as a sports photographer, you follow every play—so it's a completely different mindset.

"The other challenge is that I'm photographing him from one position. Do I focus on defense, at that end of the court? Or take a spot under the basket as he comes toward me on offense? I'm just looking for great action shots."

Souza and his Canon 5D Mark II also wound up capturing many basketball images beyond the action. "Basketball is clearly his sport of choice," he said. "It shows when he's around a basketball or a basketball player. Whether it's [Los Angeles Clippers star] Chris Paul, or

it's [Secretary of Education] Arne Duncan's son, who's all of 10 or 11, he's just very comfortable handling a basketball or talking basketball."

When asked, Souza was reluctant to nominate a favorite POTUS-and-basketball picture. "I try to think that today or tomorrow is the day I'm going to take my best photograph," he said. "It keeps me going." But a couple of memorable shots came to mind.

One is the photo that opens Chapter 1, which was taken during one of Obama's clear-the-head forays over to the White House court to play H-O-R-S-E with Reggie Love. Souza likes it, he said, "because of the lighting and casualness. He still has a tie on, and dress shoes, but there's the afternoon light, and he's flipping the ball up with a big smile. I just like the lighting and the mood—very casual."

The other, taken midway through Obama's second term and shown on the facing page, is of the president with Paul at an event for the White House's My Brother's Keeper initiative in support of young minority men. Just before Souza snapped the image, Paul confided in him how nervous he was about introducing the president. "That he was so nervous struck me as odd," Souza recalled. "Here was a guy who performed in front of tens of thousands of people. Then the president came over to loosen him up, and the result is captured in that moment. Even though the event had nothing to do with basketball, I managed to get a hoop in the background. It speaks to the president's relationship with basketball players." ∎

· ·

Facing page: Souza found that Obama kindled to life in the presence of basketball, whether handling a ball, interacting with players, or playing the game himself. Here, at a town hall for the White House's My Brother's Keeper initiative, POTUS shares a moment with Los Angeles Clippers guard Chris Paul, who also served on the President's Council on Fitness, Sports and Nutrition. (Pete Souza/The White House.)

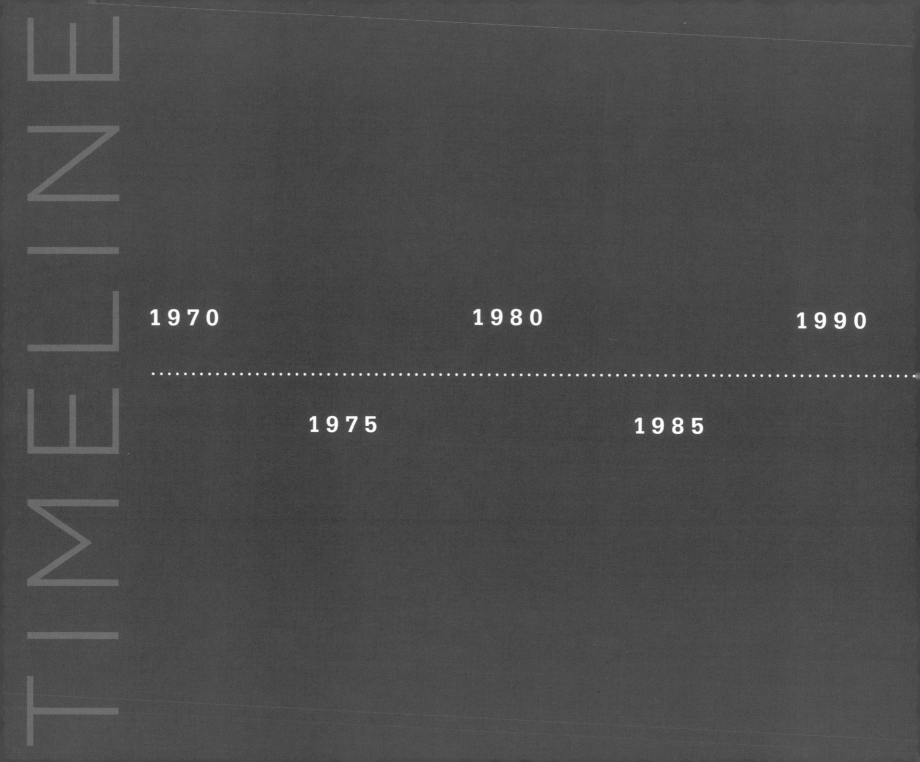

2000

2010

1995

2005

2015

TIMELINE

1971

December 1971

Barack Obama Sr. gives his son a basketball as a Christmas gift during a holiday visit to Hawaii. It's the last time young Barack sees his father, who will die in a car accident in Kenya eleven years later. In 2009 Obama will say, "The degree to which I came to love basketball—it wasn't until much later in life that I realized, 'Actually, he *gave* me that basketball.' I think there was some cause and effect there.'"

1972

Early 1972

Barry's grandfather Stan Dunham takes him to a University of Hawaii game featuring "the Fabulous Five," which is on its way to the school's first NCAA berth. Obama will write of how he identified with the team's five black starters: "I decided to become part of that world, and began going down to a playground near my grandparents' apartment after school."

(Photo: Courtesy of the University of Hawaii.)

1976

June 1976

As a Punahou School freshman, Obama signs the yearbook of Tony Peterson, the only black senior on campus, with an endorsement of Peterson's desire to become a lawyer: "Some day when I am an all-pro basketballer, and I want to sue my team for more money, I'll call on you."

September 1976

St. Martin's Press publishes *Heaven Is a Playground,* Rick Telander's account of a summer spent on the courts of Brooklyn immersed in the basketball subculture. A teenage Barry Obama picks it up, and in 2005, at a D.C. town hall in front of several hundred Illinois residents, the senator will call it "the best book on basketball I've ever read."

1977–1978

Winter 1977–1978

During a morning practice on what he'll years later call "one of those magical days," Obama, then sixteen, throws down the first dunk of his life. "This friend of mine, Larry Tavares—I still remember, but of course he wouldn't—he was shagging balls for me and I said, 'You know what? I bet I can dunk today. I'm feeling good,'" he will recall. "I took it and went *whump*—and did it about two more times. And that was about it."

1979

March 1979

At the end of Obama's senior season at Punahou, the Buff 'n' Blue win a Hawaii state basketball title with a 60–28 defeat of Moanalua High. In his accustomed role off the bench, Obama plays good defense and scores on a breakaway layup.

(Image: *Honolulu Star-Advertiser* and Hawaii State Library.)

Fall 1979

After enrolling at L.A.'s Occidental College, Obama shows up for informal basketball workouts that fall and continues to haunt Rush Gym as a pickup player even though he would apparently never play on the team. Years later Occidental's jayvee coach that season, Mike Zinn, will swear that Obama played for him—but the future president isn't in the team photo, no stat sheet or scorebook has turned up to document that he suited up, and Obama himself will say that he never played at Occidental. (Photo by Marc Campos, Occidental College photographer.)

1982

November 1982

From Manhattan, where he's now an undergraduate at Columbia, Obama writes in a letter to a girlfriend: "With every person one meets, one is presented with a weakening of one's certainty, a shakedown of the habits and grooves of separate existence. A challenge which most people react to by fear or flight. . . . [The challenge] lies in forging a unity, mixing it up, constructing the truth to be found between the seams of individual lives. All of which requires breaking some sweat. Like a good basketball game. Or a fine dance."

Late 1980s

Late 1980s

A fellow student at Harvard Law School, Hill Harper, who will go on to star in the TV series *CSI: New York,* arranges for a team representing the Black Law Students Association to travel to the state penitentiary in Walpole, Massachusetts, to play a team of inmates. The game takes place in a basement gym with guards ringing the court. The law students lose; as Harper will point out, winning might not have been worth it.

1990

Spring 1990

Michelle Obama asks her brother, Craig Robinson, to discreetly assess the character of the man she has been dating for a year by taking him along for a game with his friends. Obama passes the test during a full-court indoor run on a Saturday morning. The game includes two former Ivy League captains: Harvard's Arne Duncan, who will become Obama's secretary of education, and Robinson's former teammate at Princeton, John Rogers, who will become a fundraiser and member of both Obama inauguration committees.

2004

July 2004

As the party's candidate for a Senate seat from Illinois, Obama first comes to widespread national attention at the Democratic National Convention with a keynote speech he sketched out in a hotel room while watching the *NBA on TNT.* Several hours before taking the dais at Boston's Fleet Center, he tells a reporter, "I'm LeBron, baby. I can play on this level. I got some game."

Fall 2004

Michael Jordan, who declined to publicly support black Democrat Harvey Gantt for a North Carolina Senate seat in 1990, contributes to Obama's campaign for a vacant seat from Illinois. Obama will later say that, when the donation came in, "I wasn't sure whether I should cash the check or frame it."

2007

Spring 2007

Matt Rodriguez, the "Obama for America" director for New Hampshire, suggests that the candidate and his staff play basketball against local teams to build relationships with voters. In the campaign's first game Team Obama goes out to a large lead against a group of firefighters in Hampton, New Hampshire. "Let's just settle down a little bit," Obama tells his personal aide, former Duke captain Reggie Love, so the campaign doesn't alienate the people whose support they're trying to win.

November 2007

At the Iowa Democratic Party's Jefferson-Jackson Dinner, Obama mounts the dais with the Chicago Bulls' pregame introductory music—"Sirius," by the Alan Parsons Project—playing behind the voice of Ray Clay, the team's P.A. announcer during the Jordan years. "From our neighboring state of Illinois," Clay says, "a six-foot-two-inch force for change, Senator Barack Obama!"

December 2007

While in Spencer, Iowa, campaigning in advance of that state's caucuses, Obama twice beats Scott Price of *Sports Illustrated* one-on-one. At one point he takes the brunt of a hard foul as Secret Service agents look on. "Believe me," he tells Price, "you can get shot for doing that."

2008

January 2008

Because Iowa law prohibits electioneering on the day of the caucuses, the candidate suggests that staff and Secret Service play pickup ball with friends who have flown in for the day. Obama wins Iowa, then loses New Hampshire after failing to play, and superstitiously insists that they play on every primary day thereafter. They play, and they win—with the exception of Nevada, where they don't play and lose.

In Concord, New Hampshire, hours after his victory in Iowa, Obama says, "At some point people have to stop asserting that because I haven't been in the league long enough, I can't play. It's sort of like Magic Johnson or LeBron James who keep on scoring 30 and their team wins. But people say they can't lead their team because they're too young." Five days later Obama will lose the New Hampshire primary to Hillary Clinton.

April 2008

Obama scrimmages with the University of North Carolina varsity in Chapel Hill. He plays only five minutes, but photos of him pulling up in the lane to shoot a jumper over the Tar Heels' 6'9" Tyler Hansbrough go viral.

May 2008

In a collision during a pickup game on the campaign trail, Illinois state treasurer and former Boston University star Alexi Giannoulias barrels into Obama on a drive and bruises one of the senator's ribs. The candidate briefly blacks out and will suffer from soreness for most of the rest of the campaign. (Photo: Courtesy of Boston University Photo Services.)

131

July 2008

With no warm-up and the cameras rolling, Obama takes and makes a three-point shot during a visit to U.S. troops at Camp Arifjan in Kuwait. "I think that's all I should do," he says afterward. "It's going to go downhill from there."
(Photo: Sgt. 1st Class Jarod Perkioniemi.)

August 2008

Asked about criticism from GOP vice presidential candidate Sarah Palin, a former high school basketball star, during the Republican National Convention, Obama says, "I've been called worse on the basketball court."

In accordance with their primary-day tradition, Obama campaign staffers arrange to play on the morning of his acceptance speech at the Democratic National Convention in Denver, only to find the candidate will take a pass. "He decided he couldn't risk getting an injury," campaign aide and longtime basketball buddy Julius Genachowski will say. "So we went ahead and played without him."
(Photo: *Anchorage Daily News* Archive 1982. Copyright © *Alaska Dispatch News*.)

September 2008

Just before the first debate with GOP candidate John McCain, aide David Axelrod asks Obama if he's nervous. "I'm a little nervous, but it's a good nervous," Obama replies. "Give me the ball; let's play the game."

October 2008

If elected, Obama vows while campaigning in Indiana, he'll replace the White House bowling alley with a basketball court. It's an appeal to hoop-obsessed Hoosiers but may also be a rueful reference to the 37 he had bowled during seven frames in Altoona, Pennsylvania, six months earlier.

California governor and former bodybuilding champion Arnold Schwarzenegger derides Obama's "scrawny little arms" in a Fox News interview. A day later Obama advisor David Axelrod issues a challenge to the Republican: "Let's get Gov. Schwarzenegger on the basketball court to see what he can do."

November 2008

On a day that begins with friends, staff, and supporters playing full-court at the Attack Athletics complex in Chicago, Obama is elected as the forty-fourth president of the United States with 365 electoral votes, including those of basketball-loving Indiana and North Carolina, the reddest states he flips to blue. In both he connected with voters by playing the game—three-on-three with campaign volunteers in Kokomo and a scrimmage with the North Carolina varsity in Chapel Hill. (Photo: Andy Katz.)

2009

January 2009

Three days after Obama's inauguration, while wearing Nike Zoom LeBron VI shoes customized with the president's name, LeBron James and his Cleveland Cavaliers beat the Golden State Warriors on James's jumper at the horn. It's the first time in James's career that he has won a game as time expired.

During confirmation hearings, Sen. Herb Kohl (D-Wisc.), owner of the Milwaukee Bucks, asks attorney general nominee Eric Holder about the state of his game. "I come from the city that produced Connie Hawkins, Kareem Abdul-Jabbar, Nate (Tiny) Archibald," Holder replies. "I learned how to play ball at P.S. 127 in Queens."

Sacramento mayor and former NBA point guard Kevin Johnson, who was also elected in 2008, declares that he would have to accept an invitation to play at the White House. But, he adds, "that would be his first mistake in office. I'd have to skunk him."

(Photo: Copyright © 2009 NBA Entertainment. Photo by Rocky Widner/NBAE/Getty Images.)

February 2009

When he shows up for NBA All-Star Weekend in New Orleans without cornrows, Allen Iverson invokes Obama's inauguration, explaining that it was time for a change.

At the House Democratic Caucus annual retreat, Rep. Jay Inslee (D-Wash.), a former player at Ingraham (Washington) High, tells Obama, "Until you bring your game to the House gym, you got nothing." To which Obama replies, "I will rain threes down on you!"

March 2009

Obama fills out an NCAA men's tournament bracket during a taping with ESPN's Andy Katz, picking North Carolina to win the title, which the Tar Heels will do. A White House "Baracketology" session with ESPN will become a March staple, with the president adding a women's bracket the following year.

Vice President Joe Biden, Obama says, "does a bunch of things that don't show up in the stat sheet. He gets that extra rebound, takes the charge, makes that extra pass." (Photo: Pete Souza/The White House.)

April 2009

Obama meets with the Archbishop of Istanbul the morning after the president's NCAA tournament pick winds up winning a national championship. "Oh, and by the way, congratulations on North Carolina," Ecumenical Patriarch Bartholomew tells him.

May 2009

In her roast at the White House Correspondents' Dinner, African American comedienne Wanda Sykes takes note of Obama's love of pickup ball. "I mean, c'mon. First black president, playing basketball. That's one step forward, two steps back."

In a commencement address at Notre Dame, Obama congratulates Hallelujah Holla Back, the winner of the campus's Bookstore Basketball Tournament, and rues the elimination from the field of a team called Barack O'Ballers. "Next year," he says, "if you need a six-foot, two-inch forward with a decent jumper, you know where I live." (Photo: Pete Souza/The White House.)

June 2009

The National Park Service completes a retrofitting of the South Lawn tennis court into a full basketball court, including two basket stanchions graced with the White House seal. (The bowling alley remains untouched.) Four months later a bipartisan team of congressmen will turn up to play against Obama and such aides as Reggie Love, Arne Duncan, Ken Salazar, Sean Donovan, and Tim Geithner. They will split the first two games and then play four more times after mixing up teams. (Photo: Pete Souza/The White House.)

July 2009

Italian prime minister Silvio Berlusconi has a half-court installed in a police compound in L'Aquila to make Obama feel at home during the G-8 Summit. The president uses it to play H-O-R-S-E with aides.

September 2009

Russian oligarch Mikhail Prokhorov announces his intention to underwrite the construction of an arena in downtown Brooklyn and become majority owner of the NBA team that will play there, the relocated New Jersey Nets. After the league's Board of Governors approves the sale, Prokhorov, an avid recreational ballplayer, announces that he will run against Russian president Vladimir Putin, who will soon become an Obama nemesis. In the 2012 election Prokhorov loses badly.

November 2009

NBA Hall of Famer and former Detroit Piston Dave Bing is elected to a full term as mayor of Detroit after having already served six months standing in for Kwame Kilpatrick, who had been jailed for perjury. Bing will choose not to run for reelection, but during his four and a half years in office the city will follow through with its bankruptcy and the stirrings of a renaissance will begin. (AP Photo/Carlos Osorio.)

December 2009

In a White House ceremony Obama recognizes Wat Misaka, a Japanese American who starred at Utah and served in the U.S. Army during World War II even as his family was confined to an internment camp. Misaka played three games for the New York Knicks in 1947 to become the NBA's first nonwhite player.

2010

January 2010

Republican Scott Brown, a former Tufts University guard who ran as an opponent of the Affordable Care Act, wins the special election to fill the vacancy created by the death of Sen. Edward Kennedy (D-Mass.), a longtime champion of health-care reform. Brown's victory briefly appears to doom the chances for Obamacare to become law.

Pointing out that a quarter of the teams in the previous NCAA men's basketball tournament failed to graduate at least 30 percent of their players, Secretary of Education Arne Duncan delivers a blistering speech to the NCAA Convention in Atlanta, calling on schools to meet a more stringent academic progress rate (APR) standard or face ineligibility for postseason play. A year later the NCAA will raise its minimum, and in 2013 UConn will have to sit out the men's basketball tournament as a result. (Photo: Courtesy of Tufts University.)

February 2010

MTV airs an episode of its reality series *The Buried Life* in which the four cast members make a road trip to Washington to try to cross off what they call "the most ambitious item" on their bucket list, "Play basketball with Obama." They meet with members of Congress and cabinet officials but get no closer to their goal than a few swapped e-mails with presidential aide Reggie Love. But on a return trip to D.C. the following spring, Love will arrange for the four to shoot with the president on the White House court, where they ask Obama the show's signature question, "What do you want to do before you die?" His response: Host *SportsCenter*. (Photo: Screen capture from MTV.)

March 2010

Trey Grayson, a candidate for a U.S. Senate seat from Kentucky, airs a TV ad with a clip of his GOP primary opponent saying, "I'm Rand Paul, and I'm a Duke Blue Devil." Grayson adds, "I'm proud to say I'm a University of Kentucky Wildcat." Paul, who will win the primary and general election, releases a statement expressing his amusement at "watching my Harvard-educated opponent complain about where I went to medical school."

April 2010

Following Duke's 61–59 defeat of *Hoosiers*-knockoff Butler in an NCAA title game that comes down to a missed three-pointer that glances off the rim, Obama breaks with precedent, placing congratulatory phone calls to both victorious Blue Devils coach Mike Krzyzewski and Brad Stevens, coach of the losing Bulldogs.

The cover of *Bloomberg BusinessWeek* features Obama stroking a jump shot alongside a billing that reads, "THE HOT HAND: OBAMANOMICS IS WORKING BETTER THAN YOU THINK."

(Photo [*above*]: Pete Souza/The White House. Bloomberg *BusinessWeek* cover [*right*]: Used with permission of Bloomberg L.P. Copyright © 2015. All rights reserved.)

May 2010

With star guard Steve Nash calling Arizona's anti-immigrant law, S.B. 1070, "very misguided," and team owner Robert Sarver pledging support for Nash and his teammates, the Phoenix Suns take the floor on Cinco de Mayo wearing jerseys that read "LOS SUNS" in solidarity with the state's Latino population.

June 2010

The Chicago Bulls hire Boston Celtics assistant Tom Thibodeau as their new head coach after owner Jerry Reinsdorf is lobbied to do so by secretary of education and former Chicago public schools chief Arne Duncan, who had played at Harvard when Thibodeau served as an assistant there. Reinsdorf will later reveal that both Obama and senior advisor David Axelrod, a longtime Bulls season-ticket holder, personally complimented him on hiring Thibodeau.

July 2010

Justin Friedlander, a fourteen-year-old with an inoperable brain tumor, shoots hoops with the president on the White House court. After having been diagnosed sixteen months earlier, he embarked on "Justin's Quest" to raise awareness and funds by taking 63,000 shots—one for every person diagnosed with a primary brain tumor in the United States each year. Justin will complete his quest the following February, during a practice at NBA All-Star Weekend in Los Angeles, when the Lakers' Pau Gasol hoists him for a dunk. (Photo: Pete Souza/The White House.)

August 2010

Love, White House aide Michael Strautmanis, and longtime Obama friend Marty Nesbitt arrange a round-robin tournament at Washington's Fort McNair to celebrate the president's forty-ninth birthday. Obama helps pick the four teams, which consist of friends and aides, with such pros as LeBron James, Dwyane Wade, Carmelo Anthony, Kobe Bryant, Chauncey Billups, Pau Gasol, Chris Paul, Alonzo Mourning, Etan Thomas, Shane Battier, and Grant Hill distributed among them. As Wounded Warriors and teenage boys in the White House mentoring program look on, WNBA star Maya Moore winds up as the game's second-leading scorer, and Obama sinks a three-pointer over Derrick Rose to secure the last of his team's three victories.

November 2010

Trying to clear space with the ball while Obama crowds him during a morning pickup game at Fort McNair, Ray Decerega, director of leadership programs for the Congressional Hispanic Caucus Institute, inadvertently strikes the president in the lip with an elbow. The blow opens up a wound that will require twelve stitches to close.

December 2010

A temporary basketball court, laid down in the cafeteria at CIA headquarters in Langley, Virginia, serves as the site of a three-on-three tournament staged to benefit the federal government's holiday charity drive. CIA director Leon Panetta's team, one of forty to compete, winds up winning the title game.

2011

January 2011

After several instances of whispering in the coach's ear—"I'm just a busybody," the president says—Obama joins Love to assist with the Vipers, the fourth-grade team on which his daughter Sasha plays. Obama and Love can't make every game, but in one, the Vipers defeat the top team in the league by two points. "As long as I was always expressing love and appreciation when they did something right, they didn't mind when you said that, 'You know what? You screwed up on that one,'" the president will say. "Particularly if you used a sense of humor about it."

February 2011

Milwaukee Bucks guard and player representative Keyon Dooling denounces the Wisconsin legislature for passing a bill that strips the state's public-sector employees of collective-bargaining rights. "Wisconsin's workers deserve better," he says in a statement. "Today, our union stands proudly with our fellow union members throughout the state as they continue their fight."

May 2011

Members of U.S. Navy Seal Team Six kill Osama bin Laden during a raid on the Al Qaeda leader's compound in Pakistan, even after the crash of a helicopter forces the commandos to improvise. Seal Matt Bissonnette, a.k.a. Mark Owen, will credit their adaptability to skills developed by playing basketball among themselves. "Shoot, move and communicate," he says. "When something goes sideways, we're able to play the pickup basketball and just kind of read off each other."

During a commencement address at the University of Northern Iowa, Michelle Obama invokes the name of the basketball player whose three-point shots had led the Panthers to an upset of Kansas during the 2010 NCAA tournament. "I want you to think of two words that showed this country that young people here at UNI have got what it takes," she told a crowd of sixteen thousand students and their friends and families. *"Ali Farokhmanesh!"* (Photo [*above left*]: Screen capture from CBS. Photo [*left*]: Nelson Chenault—*USA TODAY* Sports.)

August 2011

Former NBA and UTEP star Tim Hardaway adds his voice in support of El Paso mayor John Cook and two city representatives targeted in a recall election for having endorsed domestic partner benefits for gay and lesbian couples. In 2007 Hardaway had said, "I hate gay people" after learning of the coming-out of former NBA player John Amaechi. But Hardaway now invokes El Paso's pioneering role in 1966, when the school's forerunner, Texas Western, won an NCAA title with five black starters. "It's not right to not let the gays and lesbians have equal rights here," he says. (Photo [*facing page, lower right*]: UTEP Athletics.)

November 2011

After a state dinner at Parliament House in Canberra, Obama meets Australian guard Patty Mills of the Portland Trail Blazers, who is playing for a club team in Melbourne because of the NBA lockout. "We've got to do something about this lockout," Obama tells him, to which Mills replies, "I don't know what I can do. What about you?"

2012

February 2012

New York Knicks guard Jeremy Lin touches off global curiosity by scoring more points in his first five starts, 136, than any player in NBA history. Obama boasts that he had long known about Lin, a product of Harvard, where Obama went to law school and for which his friend Arne Duncan, the secretary of education, played.

In remarks to the Democratic Governors Association, Obama alludes to a recent NBA regular-season game to describe how his campaign intends to frustrate the presumptive GOP nominee, Mitt Romney, in the general election. "We're the Miami Heat," he says. "And he's Jeremy Lin."

After leaving his house in Sanford, Florida, at halftime of the NBA All-Star Game, an unarmed black teenager wearing a hoodie is shot dead by a neighborhood watch leader. In the following days members of the Miami Heat will show solidarity with the victim, a Heat fan named Trayvon Martin, by tweeting out a picture of the entire team in hoodies, and Obama will say of the dead teen, "If I had a son, he'd look like Trayvon." (Photo: LeBron James [@KingJames] via Twitter.)

March 2012

British prime minister David Cameron joins Obama on Air Force One to fly from Washington to Dayton for a first-round NCAA tournament game between Western Kentucky and Mississippi Valley State. The two sit courtside, eat hot dogs, and at halftime do a joint standup with broadcaster Clark Kellogg.

May 2012

Obama awards the Presidential Medal of Freedom to former Tennessee women's basketball coach Pat Summitt, citing both her public battle with dementia and pioneering work on behalf of women in sports. Summitt, Obama says, paved the way for his daughters, "who are tall and gifted. They're standing up straight and diving after loose balls and feeling confident and strong."

August 2012

At the Republican National Convention in Tampa, the senator widely regarded as the best player in the upper chamber, John Thune (R-S.D.), allows that he doesn't know if he could beat the president one-on-one. "But I can tell you this," Thune says. "President Obama would be easy to defend, because you know he's always going to go to his left."

October 2012

As Obama readies for his first debate with GOP presidential candidate Mitt Romney, debate prep chief Ron Klain urges him to emulate former NBA and college coach Paul Westhead's run-and-stun offense: Look to score as many points as possible without worrying about defending Romney's shots. Obama reluctantly agrees, and fares so poorly that the cover of the next issue of *The Week* features a cartoon of Romney posterizing him with a slam dunk. Afterward Klain admits that "he was right and we were wrong," and Obama promises "a more physical style" in the next debate.

NBA commissioner David Stern says that Obama "isn't as good as he thinks he is" on the basketball court. "He's a lefty and goes the same way every time," Stern says. "I'm a loyal Democrat. A passionate Democrat. He's not as good as he thinks he is." (Image: Used with permission of *The Week* Publications, Inc. All Rights Reserved.)

November 2012

On the morning of the day he wins a second term, Obama returns to Chicago for another Election Day run, this time involving two teams instead of four. Obama's side, which includes former Chicago Bulls great Scottie Pippen as the president's first pick and Alexi Giannoulias in a supporting role, wins easily. The reversible jerseys read, "4 MORE YEARS." (Photo: Andy Katz.)

December 2012

Winthrop coach Pat Kelsey broaches the school shootings at Sandy Hook Elementary School in Newtown, Connecticut, during a press conference following a loss at Ohio State. He specifically calls on Obama and House Speaker John Boehner (R-Ohio) to enact some sort of legislation. "I didn't vote for President Obama," he says. "But you know what? He's my president now. He's my leader. I need him to step up. . . . We *gotta* change." Obama endorses a law to expand background checks that has overwhelming public support and will be introduced in the Senate, but the bill goes nowhere.

(Photo: Screen capture from ESPN.)

January 2013

In welcoming the 2012 NBA Champion Miami Heat to the White House, Obama accepts from LeBron James a basketball signed by the team and then invites James to make a few remarks by saying, "It's your world, man."

March 2013

Dennis Rodman, back from his first trip to North Korea and appearing on ABC's *This Week,* tells host George Stephanopoulos that ruler Kim Jong-un "wants Obama to do one thing, call him." Rodman adds: "[Kim] loves basketball. And I said the same thing, I said, 'Obama loves basketball.' Let's start there."

While picking Notre Dame as a second-round loser in his NCAA tournament bracket, Obama derides the team's bright green uniforms. "I am wearing a green tie today because we've got the Irish prime minister visiting," Obama explains. "But that neon glow thing wasn't working for me." Irish coach Mike Brey responds by sending the White House a Notre Dame jersey graced with "OBAMA 44." "For his next pickup game," Brey explains in a tweet. "Guarantee he'll dribble better right-handed."

The First Lady ✓
@FLOTUS

So proud of you, Jason Collins! This is a huge step forward for our country. We've got your back! -mo

RETWEETS FAVORITES
6,501   3,143

2:06 PM - 29 Apr 2013

April 2013

After NBA forward Jason Collins announces in a *Sports Illustrated* cover story that he's gay, the president telephones him with support and the First Lady sends out an encouraging tweet. Collins becomes the first active male athlete in a major American professional team sport to come out of the closet.

Tossing up shots unguarded at the White House Easter Egg Roll, Obama goes 2-for-22 in front of the cameras. On ESPN's *Pardon the Interruption,* co-host Tony Kornheiser calls it "the most embarrassing moment of his entire presidency." Two days later, at a Democratic fundraiser, party patron Tom Steyer nonetheless describes the donors in the room as "the big, not very talented guys who set the picks" so "the best left-handed shameless gunner in the world" can take the big shots. Three months later Obama will lament, "My shot's broke. It's my elbow. It's my age. I get the chicken wing." (Photo [*above*]: Michelle Obama [@FLOTUS] via Twitter. Photo [*right*]: Pete Souza/The White House.)

June 2013

During a visit to the Silicon Valley home of venture capitalist Vinod Khosla, Obama becomes fascinated by the award-winning work of two Stanford students, Muthu Alagappan and Khosla's son Neal. Using software developed by a Silicon Valley startup that can analyze complex data sets, they show the president how basketball has evolved to encompass not five but ten distinct positions, including "three-point ballhandlers" and "mid-range big men."

July 2013

Fifty years after Loyola's 1963 NCAA championship, Obama welcomes to the Oval Office the seven surviving members of that team, which featured four black starters. The Ramblers won the so-called Game of Change en route to the title, defeating the all-white Mississippi State Bulldogs, who snuck out of the state under cover of darkness in defiance of a court order preventing them from playing integrated opponents. Team captain Jerry Harkness gives Obama a framed photo of the pregame handshake between Harkness and his Bulldogs counterpart, Joe Dan Gold.

August 2013

Obama again celebrates his birthday by playing ball, this time with friends from high school and college. On *The Tonight Show* he calls the occasion "a sad state of affairs. A bunch of old guys. Where is the Ibuprofen and all that stuff?"

September 2013

Obama names as his under secretary of state for public diplomacy and public affairs the managing editor of *Time,* Richard Stengel, who was a guard on the Princeton team that won the 1975 NIT.

October 2013

Under the Affordable Care Act, Americans may enroll in health-insurance plans for a six-month period that begins this month and will coincide with the NBA regular season. The administration advertises the Obamacare exchanges during NBA games and on basketball websites to better reach young people, minorities, and single men—the demographic groups on whose broad participation the law's success will depend.

On a swing through Boston to promote the Affordable Care Act, Obama is given an advance look at a statue of Bill Russell that will be unveiled two days later. In 2011, when he presented the former Boston Celtics center with the Presidential Medal of Freedom, Obama had suggested that the city erect just such a statue. Russell's strength and dignity during the sixties, Obama said then, shaped the perceptions of black Americans in ways that helped make his own presidency possible.

November 2013

Obama honors former North Carolina basketball coach Dean Smith with the Presidential Medal of Freedom in a White House ceremony, citing Smith's support for integration in the Tar Heel State during the early sixties. Smith suffers from a progressive neurocognitive disorder, so his wife, Dr. Linnea Smith, makes the trip to accept on his behalf.

During a private meeting in Glendale, California, with entertainment executives, Obama says, "At least I know what I want to do when I retire . . . host ESPN *SportsCenter*'s Top 10 list." After making the comment, he turns expectantly to Disney CEO Bob Iger, whose company owns the cable sports network.

January 2014

Asked about terrorist groups in the Middle East other than Al Qaeda, such as ISIS, Obama minimizes them. "If a jayvee team puts on Lakers uniforms," he says, "that doesn't make them Kobe Bryant." Eight months later Obama will decide to commit U.S. military support to combat ISIS's advance in Iraq and Syria.

To promote the Obamacare exchanges, the administration unveils two new TV spots featuring former NBA greats who survived sudden health scares. Both Magic Johnson, who was diagnosed as HIV positive, and Alonzo Mourning, who had to interrupt his career for a kidney transplant, urge viewers to sign up for coverage under the Affordable Care Act. (Photo [*above left*]: Pete Souza/The White House. Photo [*right*]: Screen capture from HealthCare.gov.)

February 2014

At the Celebrity Game over NBA All-Star Weekend, Secretary of Education Arne Duncan, at age forty-nine, wins the MVP award for a performance that includes twenty points, eleven rebounds, and six assists, including a blind, over-the-shoulder flip to a cutting Skylar Diggins for a layup.

"I wanna take on Obama in Congress," says former Purdue star Curt Clawson, a GOP candidate for the open seat in Florida's Nineteenth Congressional District. "So why not start on the court? . . . He's been missing a lot lately, and not just in basketball. So, Mr. President: My house or yours?" Clawson will win the primary and, in November, the general election. (Photo [*above left*]: Screen capture from CurtClawson.com. Photo [*right*]: Copyright © 2014 NBA Entertainment. Photo by Joe Murphy/NBAE/Getty Images.)

March 2014

During a presidential visit to Brussels, the Belgian government gives Obama a life-sized, custom-baked cookie that depicts him dribbling a basketball. The cookie, made from a gingerbread-like dough called *speculaas,* was destroyed according to Secret Service protocols that apply to all gifts to the First Family of food or drink. (Photo: Margo Tilborghs.)

April 2014

UMass guard Derrick Gordon comes out after teammates tease him about an image of himself at a gay bar that he had posted and liked on Instagram. Seven months later he will become the first man to play in a Division I basketball game while openly gay.

May 2014

The WNBA becomes the first pro sports league in the United States to launch an integrated marketing program pitched to the LGBT community, with CoverGirl cosmetics as lead sponsor. The league counts 25 percent of its fan base as lesbian, as well as one of its all-time greats, Sheryl Swoopes, and most promising young stars, Brittney Griner.

Playing on a team with recent college players Craig Moore (Northwestern), Jitim Young (Northwestern), and Mack Darrow (Princeton), Arne Duncan wins USA Basketball's men's three-on-three title and the right to represent the United States in the FIBA 3x3 World Championships in Moscow. He can't go because of scheduling conflicts. (Logo used with permission of WNBA.)

June 2014

Politico reports that Obama hasn't left the White House to play basketball since November 2013: "Although he'll still shoot hoops on the grounds, he doesn't do it as often as he once did, the casualty of too many aches and injuries." The report also quotes Alonzo Mourning, who has become a frequent golfing partner. The president "expressed concern about possibly getting hurt," Mourning says. "He didn't want to do the State of the Union speech on crutches or with a broken nose."

August 2014

To celebrate his fifty-third birthday, Obama and a small circle of friends play a round-robin three-on-three tournament at Camp David. It will be the president's only non–South Lawn action in more than a year.

October 2014

Asked about Obama's golf game, Michael Jordan calls the president "a hack" and "a shitty golfer." "There is no doubt that Michael is a better golfer than I am," Obama responds. "Of course if I was playing twice a day for the last 15 years, then that might not be the case." And he alludes to the NBA team Jordan owns, which is in the process of changing its name: "You know, he might want to spend more time thinking about the Bobcats—or maybe the Hornets, but that's another issue."

Army senior Max Lenox, born in Philadelphia to a crack-addicted mother and raised as the adopted son of two gay fathers, is voted basketball captain by his West Point teammates for the second year in a row. (Photo [*facing page, bottom*]: Army Athletic Communications.)

November 2014

In remarks to the Association of the United States Army, Duke coach Mike Krzyzewski implicitly criticizes Obama's decision not to use ground troops against ISIS. "The fact that we're a free country, and we don't play home games here, is a result of having boots on the ground," he says.

A senior fellow at the Council on Foreign Relations urges Obama to play less golf and more basketball following the Democrats' losses in the midterm elections. "Basketball demands all of the qualities that make a good leader," argues Edward Alden, an expert on trade, immigration, and international economics who plays both sports. "Golf undermines them."

At a cabinet meeting three days after the midterms, Obama distributes a card to everyone in the room that reads, "We are entering the fourth quarter, and really important things happen in the fourth quarter." Soon he will strike a climate deal with China, defer deportation of millions of illegal immigrants, and launch a diplomatic opening with Cuba—moves that, with an improving economy, will help nudge his approval rating into net-positive territory.

December 2014

Asked for his assessment of Obama's performance in office, comedian Chris Rock says, "Everybody wanted Michael Jordan, right? We got Shaq. That's not a disappointment. You know what I mean? We got Charles Barkley. It's still a Hall of Fame career."

At a U.S. Marines Toys for Tots charity event, Obama helps sort holiday gifts into bins marked by gender. "You know what?" he says, placing a basketball into a box marked "GIRLS." "I want to make sure some girls play some ball."

The Chicago Bulls' Derrick Rose goes through warm-ups before a home game while wearing a black T-shirt that reads "I Can't Breathe," in memory of Eric Garner, who was choked to death while being detained by New York City police. The gesture soon spreads to college basketball, and other protests encompass victims of the police besides Garner. NBA commissioner Adam Silver frowns on the forum Rose chose to make his statement but says, "Credit to him. . . . He knew how much more effective that would be, as opposed to talking to a reporter after the game."

2015

January 2015

At the funeral Mass for former New York governor Mario Cuomo, current governor Andrew Cuomo delivers a eulogy for his father that invokes their passionate games at the State Police gym in Albany. "We tried using State Troopers as referees, but they were afraid of angering my father," he says. "That with one wrong call they would wind up on a weigh station somewhere up on the Northway. We tried letting the trooper be anonymous so there was no fear of retaliation. But the troopers also wanted to be able to wear a gun after one was attacked, by my father or myself, I can't recall which now, for making a bad call."

During an event in the East Room honoring the 2014 NBA Champion San Antonio Spurs, Obama says, "If you guys need any tips on winning back-to-back, you know where to find me."

Hall of Fame center Kareem Abdul-Jabbar, who featured in the will.i.am *Yes We Can* music video that touted the candidate during Obama's 2008 campaign, appears with the president at a White House event to urge that $215 million in support for precision medicine, including genomic data analysis and drug trials, be included in the federal budget. Since being diagnosed with leukemia in 2008, Abdul-Jabbar has been able to lead a relatively normal life thanks to targeted therapies. "The strides we're making are amazing," he will say. "Doors are starting to open up. The good thing is that Republicans are on board too, saying, yes, this is a worthy cause." (Photo: Steve Jacobs/*Times-Union* Archive.)

March 2015

With the president's niece Leslie Robinson playing forward off the bench, Princeton's Ivy League Champion women's team finishes its regular season with a 30–0 record and wins its first NCAA tournament game in history, defeating Wisconsin–Green Bay at Maryland's Cole Field House as Uncle Barack looks on. But two days later, in spite of the attendance of Supreme Court justices Elena Kagan and Sonia Sotomayor, both Princeton graduates, the Tigers are eliminated by the top-seeded Terrapins.

April 2015

Responding to pressure from both the NCAA, which is headquartered in Indianapolis and routinely hosts Final Fours there, and the NBA, which includes the state's Indiana Pacers, the Indiana legislature and Gov. Mike Pence alter the state's recently passed Religious Freedom Restoration Act so it doesn't permit discrimination against gay, lesbian, and transgender individuals.

After declining to make any NCAA tournament picks during his unsuccessful 2012 campaign for president because "I'm not plugged in well enough," Mitt Romney finishes in the 99.9th percentile among entrants in ESPN's Tournament Challenge. He correctly forecasts six of the Elite Eight and all three games at the Final Four. Obama's bracket places him in the 39.5th percentile.

Four months after the Obama administration moves to normalize relations with Havana, the NBA and FIBA send a joint delegation to Cuba that includes retired stars Steve Nash and Dikembe Mutombo as well as former WNBA guard Ticha Penicheiro. Over four days the three conduct youth clinics and work with the men's and women's national teams of the island nation.

May 2015
Speaking at Nike's Beaverton, Oregon, campus to drum up support for the proposed Trans-Pacific Partnership trade deal, Obama says, "Let's just do it." In advance of the visit, the White House tweets out the photo that can be found on page 20 of Obama, in Nike hightops, going up for a layup as a Punahou School senior. The tweet calls him "Air POTUS."

June 2015
Speaking with Marc Maron on the podcast *WTF,* Obama says he no longer plays much basketball. "I'm not as good as I used to be," he explains, adding that he gets easily frustrated: "The guys I play with . . . they sort of pity me and sympathize with me. They tolerate me, but we all know I'm the weak link on the court—and I don't like being the weak link."

Soon after the Supreme Court sides with his administration on the Affordable Care Act and same-sex marriage and Congress votes to grant him fast-track trans-Pacific trade authority, Obama is asked if he has ever had a better week. "My best week, I will tell you, was marrying Michelle," he says. "Malia and Sasha being born, excellent weeks. There was a game where I scored 27 points. That was a pretty good week. I've had some good weeks in my life."

July 2015
Harper publishes *You Don't Have to Live Like This,* by London-based German American novelist Benjamin Markovits, which includes a basketball scene featuring a fictional President Obama. In the book the president goads guests at a private reception in Detroit to join him in shoveling snow from a driveway so they can play three-on-three. An errant presidential elbow bloodies the nose of the novel's narrator and ends the game—but not before POTUS sinks a jumper and crows, "It's raining on a snowy day!"

ACKNOWLEDGMENTS

This book was more than seven years in the making, which means it survived some twenty-six hundred days when fickle presidential approval ratings or objections like "The time for this would have been right when he took office" and "It's not really a sports book *or* a politics book" might have done the whole thing in. At the same time, this project was also a few frantic months in the making—so my first thanks go to those who had the audacity to believe all along and pulled everything together.

That list begins with my agent, Andrew Blauner, who never doubted the merit in the idea, and extends to Micah Kleit and his colleagues at Temple University Press, who threw themselves into producing something on an accelerated schedule. At Temple I thank Mary Rose Muccie, Kate Nichols, Gary Kramer, Ann-Marie Anderson, Joan Vidal, and Sara Cohen. And I thank Kim Vivier and Linda Hallinger, as well as Ariana Brogan, whose design of the proposal turned the heads even of publishers that chose to pass and so impressed Temple that the house used her concept as a starting point for the final product.

Two pros took the plunge with me. Kate Patterson brought her resourcefulness and practiced eye to finding and editing the photographs. On the text side, researcher Damon Hatheway went down paths that yielded payoff after payoff. He also critiqued and fact-checked the manuscript, although any errors of commission or omission that remain are mine.

Two others were extravagant in their generosity. Claude Johnson, founder of Baller-in-Chief.com and executive director of the Black Fives Foundation, threw open his archive of all things Obama and basketball and enthusiastically renewed our ongoing conversation about the game, the president, and the power of both. And my longtime *Sports Illustrated* colleague and fellow Blaunerite S. L. (Scott) Price shared everything he had from his December 2007 game of one-on-one with the senator in Spencer, Iowa—notes, video, photos, impressions, along with transcripts of interviews in which the candidate, Michelle Obama, and Craig Robinson each spoke insightfully about how the game figured in Barack Obama's life. Much in those interviews has never before been made public.

This book literally reflects the vision of Pete Souza, the official White House photographer. In addition to taking almost half of the pictures, he and his staff in the White House Photo Office responded with alacrity to our requests to find specific images and supply context. My thanks go out to them, and to Pete foremost. Two academics, Yago Colás of the University of Michigan and Carlo Rotella of Boston College, will see reflected in the text their thoughtful and extended responses to the original proposal, feedback for which I'm hugely grateful. And for their assists along the way, I also thank Simon Bruty, Jim Demers, Josh Earnest, Rob Fleder, Pam Fogg, Peter Greenhill, Sloan Harris, John Huey, Laurel Bowers Husain, Steve James, Andy Katz, Greg Kelly, Charlie Kireker, Bronwen Latimer, Rebecca Lobo, Terry McDonell, Tim Mennel, Jack Price, Todd Purdum, John Rogers, Julius (Juice) Rose, Steve Rushin, Jon Solomon, Chenault Taylor, Rick Telander, Jeff Tiller, Brendan Tuohey, Will Voigt, Randall Whitestone, Chuck Wielgus, Christian Wolff, Katherine Wolff, Stephanie Wolff, and Dave Zirin, as well as *SI* colleagues Karen Carpenter, Seth Davis, Paul Fichtenbaum, Chris Hunt, Brad Smith, and Chris Stone.

Finally, to undertake this kind of project—long timeline, short deadline—was bound to put my family out. Fortunately we could marvel at Wizards fan Miles Rawls, and the dubious taste of one huge Belgian *speculaas* cookie, and Joe Biden's crack—as immortal as it is recycled—"If I had your hair, I'd be President." So I thank Frank and Clara for their support and forbearance and, above all, their mom, my first reader and loving partner, Vanessa Wolff.

I first began exploring the connections between Barack Obama and basketball while on assignment for *Sports Illustrated* (*SI*) shortly after the 2008 election, at the direction of Managing Editor Terry McDonell and Articles Editor Chris Hunt. When I chose to go forward with this project, John Huey, Paul Fichtenbaum, and Chris Stone, my bosses at Time Inc. and *SI,* kindly permitted me to adapt that work. So parts of this book appeared in somewhat different form in *SI* and on SI.com during January 2009. I also repurposed a portion of a column, "United We Sit," that appeared in the October 20, 2014, issue of the magazine.

Fellow *SI* contributors Scott Price and Steve Rushin passed along transcripts of interviews they conducted—Scott in 2007 with Obama, his wife, and his brother-in-law; Steve in 2015 with UConn women's basketball coach Geno Auriemma.

Where a passage or assertion is not accompanied by an endnote, it is the result of my own reporting dating back to 2008. This includes interviews with Kareem Abdul-Jabbar, David Axelrod, Robert Carlin, Sen. Robert Casey, Rey Decerega, Jim Demers, Arne Duncan, Andrew Feldstein, Julius Genachowski, Alexi Giannoulias, Grant Hill, Arthur Jackson, Claude Johnson, Andy Katz, Reggie Love, Chris McLachlin, Patty Mills, Marty Nesbitt, Gregg Popovich, Scott Price, Craig Robinson, Matt Rodriguez, John Rogers, Julius (Juice) Rose, Evan Ryan, Maya Soetoro-Ng, Pete Souza, Rick Telander, and Dave Zirin. Otherwise, I relied on sources listed below and in the Selected Bibliography.

1: Basketball Jones

pages

1   **"fitful interior struggle"**: Barack Obama, *Dreams from My Father: A Story of Race and Inheritance* (New York: Three Rivers Press, 1995), p. 76.

2   **eight hundred rounds of golf:** Don Van Natta Jr., *First off the Tee: Presidential Hackers, Duffers and Cheaters from Taft to Bush* (New York: PublicAffairs, 2003), p. 57.

2   **left cleat marks:** Ibid., p. 59.

2   **suggested plays to Washington Redskins coach George Allen:** John Sayle Watterson, *The Games Presidents Play: Sports and the Presidency* (Baltimore: Johns Hopkins University Press, 2009), p. 1.

2   **swung by Harlem's Rucker Park:** Jesse Washington, "Barack Oballa," *Bounce,* June/July 2008.

2   **claimed to have dunked:** Van Natta, *First off the Tee,* pp. 218–219.

2   **played junior-college ball:** Watterson, *Games Presidents Play,* p. 265.

2   **his passion for the Atlanta Hawks:** Bethlehem Shoals, "The Real Baller-in-Chief: Jimmy Carter," SportingNews.com, The Baseline, June 22, 2009.

2   **Herbert Hoover's gatherings:** Paul F. Boller Jr., *Presidential Diversions: Presidents at Play from George Washington to George W. Bush* (Orlando: Harcourt, 2007), p. 224.

5   **A friend, whom JFK called his "Undersecretary of Baseball":** Ibid., p. 263.

5   **"It's touch, but it's murder":** Ibid., p. 265.

5   **finds vindication in data:** Paul Taylor and the Pew Research Center, *The Next America: Boomers, Millennials and the Looming Generational Showdown* (New York: PublicAffairs, 2014), p. 90.

5   **chose to check "black":** Ibid., p. 99.

5   **"an overtly black game":** Todd Purdum, "Raising Obama," *Vanity Fair,* March 2008.

6   **"the President of the Cool":** Ishmael Reed, "President of the Cool," *New York Times,* December 18, 2013.

6   **likened the Obama gait:** Vincent Thomas, "Obama Is So Hoops," SlamOnline.com, January 23, 2009.

6   **"He's got plenty of swagger":** Steve Nash interview with John King, CNN, February 15, 2009.

6   **"And something else, too":** Obama, *Dreams from My Father,* p. 79.

7   **"Warm up the limo, Sir":** Dan Steinberg, "The Wizards Fan Who Talked Trash to Obama," *Washington Post,* D.C. Sports Bog, March 3, 2009.

9   **"sneak up behind you"**: Obama, *Dreams from My Father,* p. 79.

9   **"I don't answer those humiliating questions"**: Ben Smith, "Boxers or Briefs, Obama Edition," Politico.com, February 27, 2008.

10   **Author Jonathan Pontell calls this latter group**: A thorough discussion of Generation Jones can be found at the website Pontell maintains, GenerationJones.com.

12   **"the hallmark game of the post-industrial age"**: Michael Mandelbaum, *The Meaning of Sports: Why Americans Watch Baseball, Football, and Basketball and What They See When They Do* (New York: PublicAffairs, 2005), p. 39.

12   **a networked sport**: Ibid., pp. 202–203.

12   **"connected the disconnected parts"**: David Maraniss, *Barack Obama: The Story* (New York: Simon and Schuster Paperbacks, 2012), p. 316.

15   **"improvisation within a discipline"**: Barack Obama interview with Bryant Gumbel, *Real Sports,* HBO, April 15, 2008.

15   **"Our individualism has always"**: Barack Obama, *The Audacity of Hope: Thoughts on Reclaiming the American Dream* (New York: Three Rivers Press, 2006), p. 55.

15   **"these twin strands"**: Ibid.

2: Hoop Dreams from His Father

17   **"beyond the given of"**: Barack Obama, *Dreams from My Father: A Story of Race and Inheritance* (New York: Three Rivers Press, 1995), p. 76.

18   **"I had watched the players"**: Ibid., p. 78.

18   **"I hadn't even remembered"**: Barack Obama interview with S. L. Price of *Sports Illustrated,* December 16, 2007.

19   **"a handful of black men"**: Obama, *Dreams from My Father,* p. 79.

19   **"no talk stink"**: Stu Glauberman and Jerry Burns, *The Dream Begins: How Hawai'i Shaped Barack Obama* (Honolulu: Watermark, 2008), p. 118.

19   **"cool head, main thing"**: David Maraniss, *Barack Obama: The Story* (New York: Simon and Schuster Paperbacks, 2012), p. 294.

19   **"living out a caricature"**: Obama, *Dreams from My Father,* p. 79.

19   **"with a consuming passion"**: Ibid., p. 78.

19   **"At least on the basketball court"**: Ibid., p. 80.

19   **"There were some issues"**: Obama interview with Price.

19   **"we had some conflict"**: Austin Murphy, "Obama Discusses His Hoops Memories at Punahou High," SI.com, May 21, 2008.

19   **listened to a black friend suggest:** Obama, *Dreams from My Father,* p. 74.

20   **"Especially in high school":** Obama interview with Price.

20   **"In retrospect I'd say":** Ibid.

20   **"[I learned about] being part of something":** Murphy, "Obama Discusses His Hoops Memories."

22   **"I had bought into a set of false assumptions":** David Mendell, "Barack Obama: Democrat for U.S. Senate," *Chicago Tribune,* October 22, 2004.

23   **That first fall he worked out:** Jerry Crowe, "Obama Honed His Skills at Occidental, on Team or Not," *Los Angeles Times,* November 10, 2008.

23   **"The greatest contribution Occidental has made":** Ibid.

23   **"What I needed was a community":** Obama, *Dreams from My Father,* p. 115.

23   **"to play on courts I'd once read about":** Ibid., p. 121.

23   **"He made the mistake of asking":** Jodi Kantor, *The Obamas* (New York: Back Bay Books, 2012), p. 243.

23   **"The brother said 'double murder'":** Melanie Eversley, "Best Supporting Actor," The Root.com, October 1, 2008.

26   **Decades later Max shared:** Tucker Max, "What It's Like to Play Basketball with Obama," HuffingtonPost.com, August 15, 2012.

26   **sometimes found himself:** Kantor, *The Obamas,* p. 243.

27   **"His desire to hear out":** Michael Lewis, "Obama's Way," *Vanity Fair,* October 2012.

Gaming the President Out

28   **"a little stiff":** Vincent Thomas, "Commish's 2008 Rewind," SlamOnline.com, January 5, 2009.

28   **"Fairly good quicks":** Ethan Skolnick, "Miami Heat, Who Will Visit White House on Monday, Already Have a Connection to Obama," *Palm Beach Post,* January 26, 2013.

28   **"I could get to the rim":** Barack Obama interview with Bryant Gumbel, *Real Sports,* HBO, April 15, 2008.

28   **"extremely lefthanded":** Craig Robinson interview with S. L. Price of *Sports Illustrated,* December 2007.

29   **rarely following his passes:** Magic Johnson interview with John King, CNN, February 15, 2009.

29   **"a solid weekend warrior":** Matthew Cooper, "Inside Obama's Basketball Game," *Men's Journal,* March 2009.

29   **no longer had a nickname:** Rick Telander, "Uh, Mr. President-elect?" *Chicago Sun-Times*, December 20, 2008.

29   **reason for the sweatpants:** Ibid.

29   **"not some doofus":** Max, "What It's Like."

30   **"blinged-up, camera-hungry":** John Heilemann, "The Low-Road Warrior," *New York*, August 1, 2008.

30   **more earthbound "white" game:** Obama interview with Gumbel.

30   **"As I've gotten older":** Obama interview with Price.

30   **"Somebody like [personal aide] Reggie":** Ibid.

30   **"I'll make you feel bad about yourself":** Barack Obama interview with Marv Albert, *NBA Tip-Off*, TNT, May 25, 2010.

30   **"With people who don't know him":** Michelle Obama interview with S. L. Price of *Sports Illustrated*, December 2007.

The First Brother-in-Law

31   **"Your boy is straight":** Craig Robinson, "B-Ball with Barack," *Time*, December 17, 2008.

31   **"If you're going to play":** Obama interview with Price.

31   **"I've known some people":** Ibid.

31   **"the most important basketball game":** Chuck Klosterman, "Craig Robinson: America's First Coach," *Esquire*, January 2009.

33   **"I may not be ready for the Kentucky job":** Craig Robinson, *A Game of Character: A Family Journey from Chicago's Southside to the Ivy League and Beyond* (New York: Gotham, 2010), p. xxv.

33   **"Any seven-footers out there":** Eamonn Brennan, "Craig Robinson Recruits at DNC," ESPN.com, September 5, 2012.

33   **recruiting hadn't been the problem:** Eamonn Brennan, "Craig Robinson's Unique Tenure Ends," ESPN.com, May 5, 2014.

3: Running Game

35   **Obama instantly grasped the wisdom:** Reggie Love, *Power Forward: My Presidential Education* (New York: Simon and Schuster, 2015), p. 75.

36   **"Reggie, we want to win":** Ibid.

38   **brought in Ray Clay:** David Axelrod, *Believer: My Forty Years in Politics* (New York: Penguin Press, 2015), p. 239.

41   **Bill Clinton playing the sax on *Arsenio Hall*:** Elizabeth Williamson, "Quietly, the President Finds That Golf Is No Slam Dunk," *Wall Street Journal*, November 25, 2009.

41   **The candidate spent only five minutes:** Richard Wolffe, *Renegade: The Making of a President* (New York: Crown, 2009), p. 204.

41   **A postelection editorial in the *Indianapolis Star*:** "Taking Page from 'Hoosiers,' Obama Played to Win Indiana," *Indianapolis Star,* December 1, 2008.

44   **"He had no business taking a shot":** David von Drehle, "For Obama, Survival Is the New Winning," *Time,* November 19, 2012.

45   **"Every time we've gotten in trouble":** Wolffe, *Renegade,* p. 231.

45   **"See, I'm not a crazy Muslim":** John Jeansonne, "How Much Did Hoops Help Obama?" *Newsday,* January 21, 2009.

45   **On the morning of the Iowa caucuses:** Jodi Kantor, *The Obamas* (New York: Back Bay Books, 2012), p. 244.

45   **Some thirty-five aides:** Wolffe, *Renegade,* p. 15.

45   **helped Obama choose the teams:** Ibid., p. 10.

"The Little Brother I Never Had"

46   **passed out on a futon at a party:** Love, *Power Forward,* pp. 43–44.

46   **stopped at the wheel of his car:** Ibid., pp. 44–45.

46   **"no task too small":** Ibid., p. 62.

46   **his "iReggie":** David Picker, "Amazing Ride Nears End for 'First Brother' Reggie Love," ABCNews.com, November 22, 2011.

46   **"little brother I never had":** Brian Williams, "Obama's 'Body Man' on Leaving White House," *Rock Center with Brian Williams,* NBC, November 28, 2011.

46   **"modified the tenor of our interactions":** Love, *Power Forward,* p. 74.

47   **served as an advisor:** Rob Crilly, "Conservatives Hire Obama's 'Chief of Stuff' for Election Campaign," *The Telegraph*, February 7, 2015.

Obama, One-on-One

50   **In his notebook afterward:** Notes from Barack Obama interview with S. L. Price of *Sports Illustrated,* December 16, 2007.

Players' Choice

51   **Baron Davis first met Obama:** Love, *Power Forward,* p. 13.

51   **Kevin Garnett of the Boston Celtics scrawled:** David Aldridge, "The Meaning of Obama: NBA Embraces New Leader's Message," NBA.com, January 19, 2009.

51   **to lead a get-out-the-vote rally:** Sherron Shabazz, "Basketball and Politics: When Obama Plays, He Wins Elections," Examiner.com, November 6, 2008.

51   **to score forty-four points:** Dave Zirin, *Game Over: How Politics Has Turned the Sports World Upside Down* (New York: New Press, 2013), p. 6.

51   **tattooed four words:** Michael Lee, "A Tattoo You Can Believe In," *Washington Post,* November 9, 2008.

51   **wearing a red velvet sports jacket:** "Rockets' Steve Francis Shows Support for Obama," *USA Today,* November 4, 2008.

51   **"how the world is global":** Aldridge, "Meaning of Obama."

51   **the Boston Celtics' Ray Allen:** Jonathan Abrams, "N.B.A. Players Gravitate to Obama's Example," *New York Times,* January 19, 2008.

51   **"same roots and the same blood":** Aldridge, "Meaning of Obama."

52   **"we're all political at some point":** Abrams, "N.B.A. Players."

52   **"our country gets better":** Aldridge, "Meaning of Obama."

4: Power, Forward

55   **"a black man in America":** Barack Obama, *Dreams from My Father: A Story of Race and Inheritance* (New York: Three Rivers Press, 1995), p. 76.

55   **"And yet, Spud Webb lives":** Ta-Nehisi Coates, "Fear of a Black President," *Atlantic,* September 2012.

56   **Through his first two years in office:** Daniel Gillion, *Governing with Words: The Political Dialogue on Race, Public Policy, and Inequality in America* (forthcoming).

56   **A nonprofit that figured:** Peter Baker, "Obama Finds a Bolder Voice on Race Issues," *New York Times,* May 4, 2015.

56   **"I don't always say it":** Rembert Browne, "Barack and Me," Grantland.com, March 9, 2015.

56   **"putting thumbs on the scale":** Ibid.

59   **On the eve of his inauguration in 1905:** Paul F. Boller Jr., *Presidential Diversions: Presidents at Play from George Washington to George W. Bush* (Orlando: Harcourt, 2007), p. x.

59   **the NBA's League Pass app loaded on his iPad:** Barack Obama interview with Bill Simmons, *B.S. Report Podcast,* Grantland.com, March 1, 2012.

59   **shot hoops in a D.C. gym:** Photographer Callie Shell captured photos of Obama shooting baskets alone in the gym at Coolidge High School in Washington, D.C., on January 19, 2009.

59   **"We're the Miami Heat":** Jodi Kantor, "The Competitor in Chief," *New York Times,* September 2, 2012.

59   **described the state of play in familiar terms:** Richard McGregor, "US Race Shapes Up as Fight to Wire," *Financial Times,* August 24, 2012.

59   **"If a jayvee team puts on Lakers uniforms":** David Remnick, "Going the Distance," *New Yorker,* January 27, 2014.

59   **"'Hey, Spain, I'm not going to start'":** Jordan Schachtel, "Duke's Coach K Delivers Scathing Critique of Obama Foreign Policy," Breitbart.com, November 5, 2014.

60   **"At Purdue, our biggest challenge":** Rep. Curt Clawson (R-Fla.), "Tea Party Response to President Obama's State of the Union Address," TeaPartyExpress.org, January 20, 2015.

60   **"watch D-Wade on *SportsCenter*":** Ethan Skolnick, "Miami Heat, Who Will Visit White House on Monday, Already Have a Connection to Obama," *Palm Beach Post,* January 26, 2013.

60   **Michelle Obama dunked a mini-basketball:** Reid Cherlin, "The Worst Wing," *New Republic,* April 7, 2014.

60   **When they learned of the administration's plan:** Jennifer Haberkorn, "Mitch McConnell Asks Pro Sports to Stay Away from Obamacare Promotion," Politico.com, June 28, 2013.

60   **"I would caution you against":** Sahil Kapur, "GOP Leaders Warn Pro Sports Leagues Not to Promote Obamacare," TalkingPointsMemo.com, June 28, 2013.

62   **for the final push to the sign-up deadline:** Freddie Allen, "President Teams Up with Athletes to Push Obamacare," NNPA News Service, March 27, 2014.

63   **HHS blasted out data:** Arpit Misra, "Common Sports Injuries: Incidence and Average Charges," ASPE.HHS.gov, March 17, 2014.

63   **the value the administration derived:** Kurt Badenhausen, "The NBA's Endorsement All-Stars 2014," *Forbes,* February 17, 2014.

63   **"In my 20s and early 30s I thought I was invincible":** Darlene Superville, "Five New Things about President Obama," Associated Press, December 2, 2013.

63   **"For all you weekend warriors":** Barack Obama interview with Colin Cowherd, *The Herd with Colin Cowherd,* ESPN Radio, December 12, 2014.

63   **"I appreciate that LeBron and Magic":** Ibid.

64   **To help repair relations with Spanish prime minister:** Jim Hoagland, "Spain's Zapatero Looking Forward to Obama's Tenure," *Washington Post,* November 23, 2008.

64   **saying, "That guy can play!":** Alexander Wolff, "How I Spent My Lockout," *Sports Illustrated,* November 21, 2011.

64   **shouted out Senegalese draft prospect Gorgui Dieng:** Office of the Press Secretary, "Remarks by President Obama and President Sall of Senegal in an Exchange of Toasts," WhiteHouse.gov, June 27, 2013.

64   **Hedo Turkoglu and Mehmet Okur had "game":** Office of the Press Secretary, "Remarks by President Obama to the Turkish Parliament," WhiteHouse.gov, April 6, 2009.

64   **Bush's having already given Kikwete:** Christopher Clarey, "World Leaders Who Could Make Obama Sweat," *International Herald Tribune,* November 17, 2008.

64   **Harper gave the president a basketball:** Tu Thanh Ha, "U.S. Releases List of Gifts Obama Received from Foreign Governments: Guess What We Sent," *Globe and Mail,* April 26, 2013.

64   **During the July 2009 G-8 summit:** Jake Tapper, "Hoopster-in-Chief Plays 'Horse' in Italy," ABCNews.com, July 9, 2009.

64   **the Belgian government gave the president:** Joe Coscarelli, "Belgium Atones for Racist Obama Caricatures with Racist Giant Cookie," NYMag.com, March 25, 2014.

64   **You could find Dallas Mavericks star Dirk Nowitzki:** Tim MacMahon, "Dirk Nowitzki Dines with Pres. Obama, German Chancellor," ESPN.com, June 19, 2013.

64   **"congratulations on North Carolina":** Jake Tapper, "Ecumenical Patriarch Congratulates President Obama on Tarheels Winning NCAA," ABCNews.com, April 7, 2009.

64   **approach to international relations that she called "smart power":** David Jackson, "Obama Team and NBA Partner on Diplomacy, Public Safety," *USA Today,* February 16, 2011.

65   **beginning in 2011:** Ibid.

67   **"I have learned from the words of Yao Ming":** Dave Cook, "Obama Cites That Great Chinese Philosopher, Yao Ming," CSMonitor.com, July 27, 2009.

67   **had dropped in on Lakers games:** Christopher Bodeen, "Chinese, U.S. Presidents Look to Strike Up Relationship at California Summit," Associated Press, May 30, 2013.

69   **"since you never know":** Kate Andersen, "Obama Invites LeBron James to Play in White House Court Opener," Bloomberg.com, June 20, 2009.

69   **"once every two or three weeks":** Barack Obama interview with Marv Albert, *NBA Tip-Off,* TNT, May 25, 2010.

71   **"He didn't want to do the State of the Union":** Jennifer Epstein, "Obama's New Teammate: Alonzo Mourning," *Politico,* June 1, 2014.

71   **"When President Obama goes back to basketball":** Elizabeth Williamson, "Quietly, the President Finds That Golf Is No Slam Dunk," *Wall Street Journal,* November 25, 2009.

71   **"politics is a blood sport"**: Edward Alden, "Obama Needs to Forget Golf and Bring Back His Basketball Hustle," *Washington Post,* November 13, 2014.

71   **he had taken to the court in a different capacity**: Jodi Kantor, *The Obamas* (New York: Back Bay Books, 2012), p. 308.

71   **"they just think of it as dad"**: Barack Obama interview with Andy Katz, espnW.com, March 26, 2012.

72   **less stem-winding motivator than technocrat**: Ibid.

72   **"want them to win so bad"**: Obama interview with Simmons.

72   **"I can't sit down and watch an entire game"**: Obama interview with Cowherd.

72   **Cable and satellite carriers that served**: Chuck Todd, *The Stranger: Barack Obama in the White House* (New York: Little, Brown, 2014), p. 388.

Baracketology

75   **hadn't yet delivered a budget**: Kevin McCarthy, "Obama Spends More Time on 'March Madness Brackets' Than 'Writing a Budget,'" HuffingtonPost.com, March 13, 2013.

75   **A typical Fox News chyron**: Thomas Bishop, "Right-Wing Madness over Obama's NCAA Tournament Bracket," MediaMatters.org, March 19, 2014.

75   **where half of the teams to make his Final Fours came from**: Todd, *The Stranger,* p. 388.

75   **Nate Silver nonetheless reverse-engineered**: Nate Silver, "Cherry-Picker-in-Chief," FiveThirtyEight.com, March 19, 2009.

76   **"The fuck wrong"**: Rodger Sherman, "NC State Player after Upsetting Villanova: 'The F*** Wrong with Barack Obama?'" SBNation.com, March 21, 2015.

76   **"had to bust your bracket!"**: Jon Meoli, "Maryland Women Celebrate with Barack Obama Cutout after Win over Princeton," *Baltimore Sun,* March 24, 2015.

76   **"not plugged in well enough"**: "President Obama Picks Tar Heels," ESPN.com, March 14, 2012.

76   **Three years later**: Jeremy Stahl, "Mitt Romney's Final NCAA Bracket Was Frighteningly Accurate," Slate.com, April 7, 2015.

76   **"I don't think anyone"**: Mark Leibovich, "Obama Seizes Chance to Score as an Everyman," *New York Times,* March 22, 2012.

Hardwood Cabinet

77   **He met his wife-to-be**: David Axelrod, *The Believer: My Forty Years in Politics* (New York: Penguin Press, 2015), p. 45.

77   **streaky outside shooting:** Richard Wolffe, *Renegade: The Making of a President* (New York: Crown, 2009), p. 50.

77   **Served as manager:** Edward L. Kenney, "Biden Still in Touch with His Claymont Roots," Wilmington (Del.) *News-Journal*, August 27, 2008.

77   **Secret Service code name:** Rex W. Huppke, "'Renegade' Joins 'Twinkle,' 'Rawhide,' 'Lancer' on List of Secret Service Code Names," *Chicago Tribune*, November 10, 2008.

78   **jumped into a half-court scrimmage:** "Tim Geithner Plays Basketball in China, Hits a 3-Pointer!" HuffingtonPost.com, May 24, 2010.

78   **was cut twice and served as manager:** Timothy F. Geithner, *Stress Test: Reflections on Financial Crises* (New York: Crown, 2014), p. 28.

78   **bruised the candidate's ribs:** Rick Pearson, "Obama Basketball Chum: President's 'A Good Finisher,'" *Chicago Tribune*, September 23, 2011.

78   **high school football star:** Melanie Eversley, "Best Supporting Actor," TheRoot.com, October 1, 2008.

78   **organized a late-eighties pickup game:** Kantor, *The Obamas,* p. 243.

79   **He also took part in the 2008 Election Day run:** Ibid.

79   **"In a school of short academic nerds":** Amy Chozick, "The Presidential Pickup Game," *Wall Street Journal,* December 19, 2008.

79   **"He's 10 years younger":** Sam Stein, "Holder: I Can't Beat Obama on Basketball Court but I Can 'Hang with Him,'" HuffingtonPost.com, February 15, 2009.

79   **versatility and soft touch:** Matthew Cooper, "Inside Obama's Basketball Game," *Men's Journal,* March 2009.

79   **preparing him for a career:** Frank Davies, "Audacity of Hoops: Obama Recruits Dream Team . . . of Basketball Players," *San Jose Mercury News,* December 22, 2008.

79   **wrap a broken ankle:** Michelle Cottle, "The Sheriff," *New Republic*, March 31, 2010.

80   **for having played golf:** Jason Horowitz, "Challenging the President . . . but Only on the Golf Course," *New York Times,* September 6, 2014.

80   **members of the "band of brothers":** Jackie Calmes, "Visits with School Pals Are a Touchstone on President's Trips to Hawaii," *New York Times*, January 3, 2014.

80   **Pfeiffer invoked Stacey King's 1990 comment:** David McCabe, "Dems Mock McConnell for Linking GOP to Positive Economy," TheHill.com, January 7, 2015.

80   **a basketball signed by Obama:** Evan Osnos, "In the Land of the Possible," *New Yorker,* December 22 and 29, 2014, pp. 94–95.

80   **At Lakeside High School in Atlanta:** Robert Sullivan, "Samantha Power Takes on the Job of a Lifetime as Ambassador to the U.N.," *Vogue,* October 14, 2003.

82   **Challenged Obama to come:** Ed O'Keefe, "Salazar Challenges Obama to Basketball Game," *Washington Post,* January 23, 2009.

82   **didn't get along with the coach:** William L. Silber, *Volcker: The Triumph of Persistence* (New York: Bloomsbury, 2012), p. 17.

82   **"It was a major event":** David Beckwith, "For the Parsimonious Head of the Federal Reserve, Squeezing the Dollar Is Policy, Pinching Pennies a Way of Making Ends Meet," *People,* May 10, 1982.

82   **"When you come up through the elite schools":** Kantor, *The Obamas,* p. 198.

83   **several women on a rec-league team:** Nicholas Lemann, "Street Cop," *New Yorker,* November 11, 2013.

83   **"People checked their knees":** Nina Burleigh, "White Power," *New York,* July 9, 2001.

83   **"The same toughness she shows":** Ben Protess, "White Says Her S.E.C. Would Be Tough on Wall St.," *New York Times,* Deal Book, March 12, 2013.

The Secretary of Schoolin' People

85   **"played with relaxed ferocity":** Carlo Rotella, "On the Basketball Court with Arne Duncan," NewYorker.com, January 25, 2010.

86   **would assume he was black:** Steve Bzomowski, "Arne Duncan, *Sec'y of Ed, the Basketball Player," HoopsTips.Wordpress.com, December 16, 2008.

86   **"Somebody always set me up":** Rotella, "On the Basketball Court."

86   **"an excuse he did not want to use":** Bzomowski, "Arne Duncan."

87   **"Arne Duncan was not a great talent":** Ibid.

Center Circles

89   **There in Room SB-322:** Meredith Shiner, "The Untold Story of the 4 O'Clock Caucus: Bipartisan Basketball in a Bygone Era," Yahoo.com, April 6, 2015.

89   **"the Four O'Clock Caucus":** Ibid.

89   **"If I ever have an opportunity":** Wright Thompson, "The Power Game," ESPN.com, *Outside the Lines,* June 10, 2009.

89   **wheezed back to life:** Ibid.

89   **"inner, inner, inner sanctum":** Ibid.

90   **virtually everyone in the gym:** Michael Lewis, "Obama's Way," *Vanity Fair,* October 2012.

90   **"Are you guys really legit?":** *The Buried Life,* Episode 95, "Playing Basketball with Obama," MTV, airdate February 22, 2010.

Lip Service

92   **the president played with a mouth guard:** Lewis, "Obama's Way."

92   **Reporters nonetheless doorstepped:** Stan Grossfeld, "Man Who Roughed Up Obama Finally Speaks," *Boston Globe,* May 6, 2013.

Ding-Dong Diplomacy

93   **anyone in the White House not already a hawk:** David Sanger, "Kenneth Bae and Matthew Todd Miller, Released by North Korea, Are Back on U.S. Soil," *New York Times,* November 8, 2014.

93   **"do me a solid":** Franz Lidz, "Where Are They Now: Dennis Rodman," *Sports Illustrated,* July 8, 2013.

93   **"His whole deal is to talk basketball":** Ibid.

93   **A State Department spokesman:** "Dennis Rodman: Kim Jong-un Wants to Talk to Barack Obama about Basketball," Associated Press via Telegraph.co.uk, March 1, 2013.

93   **"Settling accounts with the U.S.":** Ibid.

93   **"Before I landed":** Lidz, "Where Are They Now: Dennis Rodman."

93   **he would do back home "with the boss":** Nate Thayer, "25 Years of Slam Dunk Diplomacy: Rodman Trip and History of U.S.–North Korean Basketball Diplomacy," Nate Thayer.Wordpress.com, March 4, 2013.

93   **so taken by his guest's enthusiasm:** Eugene Schmiel, "Michael Jordan in North Korea (Revisited)," UNC.edu, *Foreign Diplomacy,* Fall 2000.

94   **the United States seemed to have a change of heart:** Thayer, "25 Years of Slam Dunk Diplomacy."

94   **Rodman produced a letter:** TMZ Staff, "Dennis Rodman: I Helped Kenneth Bae Get Released . . . Here's the Proof," TMZ.com, November 8, 2014.

The World's Most Elegant Locker Room

97   **a spontaneous game:** John Altavilla, "Obama Has the Range," *Hartford Courant,* April 28, 2009.

97   **photobombed him with bunny ears:** Morgan Whitaker, "Bunny Ears on the President: Inappropriate or All in Good Fun?" MSNBC.com, August 5, 2013.

97–98   **thank the North Carolina Tar Heels:** Associated Press via ESPN.com, "Tar Heels Visit White House," May 11, 2009.

98   **James called Obama "coach":** Jimmy Hascup, "LeBron James Calls President Obama 'Coach' during Visit," *USA Today,* January 29, 2013.

98 **"one of these guys starts yelling at Mario":** "Obama Jokes about Mario Chalmers Getting Yelled at by Teammates," HuffingtonPost.com, January 14, 2014.

98 **After busting the chops:** Dana Milbank, "Washington Sketch: Sports-Loving President Finds It's Not Always Fun and Games," *Washington Post,* July 28, 2009.

98 **The first took place:** Ken Belson, "At the White House, It Is Often Good Politics to Play Ball," *New York Times,* April 24, 2010.

98 **until the presidency of Ronald Reagan:** Ethan Trex, "Welcome to the White House," Grantland.com, August 12, 2011.

99 **failed to bounce back:** Skolnick, "Miami Heat."

100 **"What's fun is when the women":** Obama interview with Simmons.

100 **time to visit military families:** Kenneth T. Walsh, "Obama Prefers Public Service Component When Teams Visit White House," *U.S. News and World Report Online,* June 19, 2009.

100 **were happy to mix things up:** Ray Holloman, "Barack Obama, Lakers Give Championship Feeling to Boys & Girls Club," SFGate.com, December 13, 2010.

The Loyal Opposition

104 **known for his feisty defense:** "The G.O.P. Dream Team," *New York Times,* January 11, 2009.

104 **"John Thune is the best":** Patrick W. Gavin, "Obama v. Thune: Who's Got Game?" *Washington Examiner,* December 8, 2008.

104 **"looks like she's got some game":** Tahman Bradley, "Stephanopoulos: Obama Jokes I Could Take Palin in Basketball," ABCNews.com, September 7, 2008.

105 **"scrawny little arms":** Michael Finnegan, "A Challenge for Schwarzenegger," *Los Angeles Times,* November 2, 2008.

105 **"playing pickup basketball at Harvard":** Karl Rove, "Why Hillary Won," *Wall Street Journal,* January 10, 2008.

105 **"Allen Iverson with a Harvard Law degree":** John Heilemann, "The Low-Road Warrior," *New York,* August 1, 2008.

105 **"He's a false President":** Jonathan Easley, "Gingrich Disparages Obama, Calls Him 'Not a Real President,'" TheHill.com, September 26, 2012.

105 **"I hope he'll have a look at the video":** Curt Clawson interview with Liza Fernandez, WFTX-TV News, February 3, 2014.

105 **a noon-hoop regular:** Trip Gabriel and Richard Perez-Pena, "Campus Colleagues, Basketball Teammates, and Now, Political Rivals," *New York Times,* June 12, 2014.

105   **addressed a neo-Confederate group:** Daniel Strauss, "McDaniel Says He Only Attended One Neo-Confederate Event," TalkingPointsMemo.com, November 1, 2013.

105–106   **an editorial in his hometown newspaper:** Daniel Strauss, "Hometown Editorial: McDaniel Isn't a Racist Because He Played Basketball," TalkingPointsMemo.com, July 8, 2014.

106   **he pronounced himself "grateful":** Office of Rep. John Shimkus (R-Ill.), "Shimkus Invited to White House for Basketball Game," press release, October 8, 2009.

106   **which afterward he called "enjoyable":** Tweet from @RepShimkus, October 8, 2009.

106   **walked out of the president's address:** Andrew Greiner, "Obama Invites 'Walk Out' Shimkus to Basketball Game," NBCChicago.com, October 8, 2009.

The Inevitability of Golf

107   **"If I had my way":** H. L. Mencken, *The Days of H. L. Mencken: Happy Days, Newspaper Days, Heathen Days* (New York: Alfred A. Knopf, 1947), p. 28.

107   **"You cannot play if":** Don Van Natta Jr., *First off the Tee: Presidential Hackers, Duffers and Cheaters from Taft to Bush* (New York: PublicAffairs, 2003), p. 118.

108   **"the closest thing to":** John Harwood, "A Chance to Get Outside," *New York Times,* June 20, 2009.

108   **"a whole bunch of Secret Service":** Barack Obama interview with Harry Smith, *The Early Show,* CBS, June 23, 2009.

108   **"It's a game that I keep":** Barack Obama interview with Russia ITAR-TASS via "Russian TV Grills Obama on Heroes, Favorite Movie, His Nice Wife," *Los Angeles Times,* Top of the Ticket, July 6, 2009.

108   **the best round of his life:** Michael S. Schmidt, "The Nation's Private Golfer-in-Chief," *New York Times,* January 3, 2015.

108   **he regretted doing so:** Ibid.

108   **the D.C. pundit class:** Michael Hirsh, "Our Lonely First Duffer," *Politico Magazine,* August 7, 2014.

108   **the presidential record:** Van Natta, *First off the Tee,* p. 57.

109   **master of the thirty-six-hole workweek:** Jean Edward Smith, "The Big Question: Who Is the Most Underrated Politician in History?" *Atlantic,* November 2014.

109   **"Basketball may have more street cred":** "Obama's Golfing Is No Cause for Shame," *Economist,* November 24, 2009.

109   **"Let me put it in language":** Alex Podlogar, "Whatever Happened to Baller-in-Chief?" APodlogar.Wordpress.com, February 3, 2010.

109   **A president boxed in:** Alden, "Obama Needs to Forget Golf."

5: The Game in the Age of Obama

112 **league's consistent collection of high marks:** Racial and Gender Report Cards for the NBA, as assessed annually by the Institute for Diversity and Ethics in Sport at the University of Central Florida, may be found at Tidesport.org/racialgenderreportcard/html.

112 **Stern's response to those post-Jordan public relations challenges:** Dave Zirin, *Game Over: How Politics Has Turned the Sports World Upside Down* (New York: New Press, 2013), p. 166.

112 **"This is a huge deal":** Harvey Araton, "The Great State of the NBA Votes for Obama," *New York Times,* November 9, 2008.

113 **"The way we saw it":** "Is Basketball Slowly Replacing Soccer as Top Global Sport?" *Sports Business Daily,* December 10, 2008.

114 **Milwaukee Bucks signaled support:** National Basketball Players Association, "Statement by NBPA Executive Director Billy Hunter and First Vice-President Keyon Dooling in Opposition to Wisconsin Assembly Anti-Union Bill," NBPA.org, February 25, 2011.

114 **"Just because somebody's a sports figure":** Barack Obama interview with Marv Albert, *NBA Tip-Off,* TNT, May 25, 2010.

114 **"This is who I am, I'm proud of it":** Office of the Press Secretary, "News Conference by the President," WhiteHouse.gov, April 30, 2013.

114 **"Everything leads to the NBA for me":** Steve Buckley, "UMass Player Inspired by Jason Collins, Michael Sam," *Boston Herald,* November 14, 2014.

115 **"Magic has set the standard":** Jack McCallum, "We Believe in Magic," *Sports Illustrated,* December 15, 2014.

115 **"the country and the world to think":** Tina Daunt, "Obama Defends Affordable Care Act at Magic Johnson Fundraiser," HollywoodReporter.com, November 25, 2013.

116 **"We all know how to shoot":** Matt Bissonnette, a.k.a. Mark Owen, interview with Scott Pelley, *60 Minutes,* CBS, September 9, 2012.

116 **It's not clear that Michael Jordan:** Will Leitch, "Loud and Clear: Athletes Speaking Up," SportsOnEarth.com, December 7, 2014.

116 **The words explained why Jordan declined:** LZ Granderson, "The Political Michael Jordan," ESPN.com, August 14, 2012. **"not by raised fists":** L. Jon Wertheim and Tom Lamont, "Hoops and Dreams," *Observer* (London), January 31, 2009.

117 **predisposed to idealism and speaking one's mind:** David Burstein, "Millennials Will Save Us," Salon.com, February 16, 2013.

117   **a $2.73 million fine to settle housing discrimination charges:** Franz Lidz, "Sterling Reputation," *Sports Illustrated,* May 5, 2014.

117   **"These kids come from the same neighborhoods":** Vincent Goodwill, "Pistons Players Reflect on Teen's Death," *Detroit News,* March 28, 2012.

117   **watched a demonstration on the street:** Ben Strauss, "Derrick Rose Sees Taking a Stand as His Responsibility," *New York Times,* December 10, 2014.

117   **Regardless of his own feelings:** Adam Silver, "Political Expression and Activism in Today's NBA," panel at Princeton University, MediaCentralLive.princeton.edu, March 24, 2015.

118   **"Obviously we're not on the frontline":** Zach Schonbrun, "For LeBron James and Other Stars, the Political Is Personal," *New York Times,* December 8, 2014.

118   **Before a game against Fontbonne:** Dave Zirin, "From Rams to Ariyana Smith, Athletes Honor Michael Brown," Progressive.org, December 3, 2014.

118   **"LeBron is in your living room":** Josh Marshall, "Sports, Race and the Politics of Shirts," TalkingPointsMemo.com, December 11, 2014.

118   **"It's the Jay-Z line":** David Aldridge, "The Meaning of Obama: NBA Embraces New Leader's Message," NBA.com, January 19, 2009.

118   **"We went through a long stretch":** Sandra Sobieraj Westfall, "President Obama: More Sports Stars Should Speak Out on Social Issues," People.com, December 18, 2014.

118   **"I give a shit":** Zirin, *Game Over,* p. 6.

118   **While Jordan had supported:** Granderson, "Political Michael Jordan."

119   **"cryin' like a damn baby":** Aldridge, "Meaning of Obama."

119   **hard to distinguish him from Adam Silver:** Lee Jenkins, "Adam Silver Is His Own Man," *Sports Illustrated,* May 26, 2014.

119   **"There's a commercial side":** Silver, panel at Princeton.

119   **Soon thereafter an audiotape emerged:** Mike Tierney, "Despite Tumult around Them, the Atlanta Hawks Have Risen to the Top," *New York Times,* January 4, 2015.

121   **"I do think that":** Dave Jamieson, "Obama Calls on NCAA to Rethink the Way It Protects and Pays Athletes," HuffingtonPost.com, March 21, 2015.

121   **"A team that has 13 or 15%":** Arne Duncan interview with Bill Simmons, *B.S. Report Podcast,* Grantland.com, March 8, 2013.

121   **"The secretary indicated":** Ben Strauss, "As NCAA Issues Pile Up, a Call for a Commission," *New York Times,* December 13, 2014.

128   **gives his son a basketball:** Barack Obama, *Dreams from My Father: A Story of Race and Inheritance* (New York: Three Rivers Press, 1995), p. 106.

128   **"The degree to which":** Barack Obama interview with Oprah Winfrey, *Christmas at the White House: An Oprah Primetime Special,* ABC, December 13, 2009.

128   **"I decided to become":** Obama, *Dreams from My Father,* p. 119.

128   **"I'll call on you":** David Remnick, *The Bridge: The Life and Rise of Barack Obama* (New York: Knopf, 2010), pp. 90–91.

129   **he'll years later call:** Barack Obama interview with S. L. Price of *Sports Illustrated,* December 16, 2007.

129   **Years later Occidental's jayvee coach:** Jerry Crowe, "Obama Honed His Skills at Occidental, on Team or Not," *Los Angeles Times,* November 10, 2008.

129   **letter to a girlfriend:** David Maraniss, *Barack Obama: The Story* (New York: Simon and Schuster Paperbacks, 2012), p. 455.

130   **arranges for a team:** Jodi Kantor, *The Obamas* (New York: Back Bay Books, 2012), p. 243.

130   **not have been worth it:** Ibid.

130   **Michelle Obama asks her brother:** Craig Robinson, *A Game of Character: A Family Journey from Chicago's Southside to the Ivy League and Beyond* (New York: Gotham, 2010), p. 149.

130   **"I'm LeBron, baby":** David Mendell, *Obama: From Promise to Power* (New York: Amistad, 2007), p. 2.

130   **"cash the check or frame it":** LZ Granderson, "The Political Michael Jordan," ESPN.com, August 14, 2012.

130   **"Let's just settle down":** Reggie Love, *Power Forward: My Presidential Education* (New York: Simon and Schuster, 2015), pp. 74–75.

131   **mounts the dais:** Jeff Zeleny, "Rule No. 1: Do Not Call Him 'Ball Hog in Chief,'" *New York Times,* January 9, 2009.

131   **"get shot for doing that":** Obama interview with Price.

131   **"At some point people":** Richard Wolffe, *Renegade: The Making of a President* (New York: Crown, 2009), p. 106.

131   **The candidate briefly blacks out:** Rick Pearson, "Obama Basketball Chum: President's 'A Good Finisher,'" *Chicago Tribune,* September 23, 2011.

132   **"that's all I should do":** Kate Andersen, "Obama Invites LeBron James to Play in White House Court Opener," Bloomberg.com, June 20, 2009.

132 **"I've been called worse"**: Carolyn Lochhead, "Obama Suddenly Riled," SFGate.com, Politics Blog, September 4, 2008.

132 **"get Gov. Schwarzenegger"**: Michael Finnegan, "A Challenge for Schwarzenegger," *Los Angeles Times,* November 2, 2008.

133 **During confirmation hearings:** Sam Stein, "Holder: I Can't Beat Obama on Basketball Court but I Can 'Hang with Him,'" HuffingtonPost.com, February 15, 2009.

133 **"I'd have to skunk him"**: Zeleny, "Rule No. 1."

133 **without cornrows, Allen Iverson:** FreeDarko Presents, *The Undisputed Guide to Pro Basketball History* (New York: Bloomsbury, 2010), p. 185.

133 **"you got nothing"**: Josh Feit, "Rep. Inslee Trash Talks Obama," SeattleMet.com, June 29, 2009.

133 **"things that don't show up"**: *New York Times* via Kenneth T. Walsh, "Biden Is a Key Adviser and Confidant in Obama's White House," USNews.com, March 20, 2009.

134 **"congratulations on North Carolina"**: Jake Tapper, "Ecumenical Patriarch Congratulates President Obama on Tarheels Winning NCAA," ABCNews.com, April 7, 2009.

134 **"I mean, c'mon"**: "2009 White House Correspondents' Dinner," C-SPAN.org, May 9, 2009.

134 **"you know where I live"**: "Transcript: Obama's Notre Dame Speech," *Chicago Tribune,* May 17, 2009.

134 **"In the 2012 election Prokhorov loses badly"**: Katya Soldak, "Russian Billionaire Mikhail Prokhorov: From Oligarch to President?" *Forbes,* March 25, 2013.

135 **Pointing out that a quarter of the teams:** Eric Prisbell, "U.S. Education Secretary Duncan Urges Change for NCAA, NBA," *Washington Post,* January 15, 2010.

135 **MTV airs an episode:** *The Buried Life,* Episode 95, "Play Basketball with Obama," MTV, airdate February 22, 2010.

135 **on a return trip to D.C. the following spring:** Issie Lapowsky, "MTV's 'Buried Life' Stars Play Basketball with President Obama as One of Their Bucket List Dreams," *New York Daily News,* April 13, 2010.

136 **Trey Grayson, a candidate for a U.S. Senate seat:** Domenico Montanaro, "Rand Paul, Wrong Shade of Blue?" FirstRead.NBCNews.com, March 15, 2010.

136 **Obama breaks with precedent:** Office of the Press Secretary, "Readout of the President's Calls to Duke University Coach Mike Krzyzewski and Butler University Coach Brad Stevens," WhiteHouse.gov, April 6, 2010.

136 **Arizona's anti-immigrant law:** Dave Zirin, *Game Over: How Politics Has Turned the Sports World Upside Down* (New York: New Press, 2013), pp. 126–127.

136   **The Chicago Bulls hire:** David Jackson, "Obama and Aides Are Strong Backers of Bulls Hoops Coach," *USA Today,* March 9, 2011.

137   **Obama sinks a three-pointer:** Kantor, *The Obamas,* p. 246.

137   **A temporary basketball court:** Paul Bedard, "CIA's Panetta Brings March Madness to Langley," USNews.com, Washington Whispers, Dec. 22, 2010.

138   **"I'm just a busybody":** Barack Obama interview with Andy Katz, espnW.com, March 26, 2012.

138   **"As long as I was always":** Ibid.

138   **"Wisconsin's workers deserve better":** National Basketball Players Association, "Statement by NBPA Executive Director Billy Hunter and First Vice-President Keyon Dooling in Opposition to Wisconsin Assembly Anti-Union Bill," NBPA.org, February 25, 2011.

138   **"Shoot, move and communicate":** Matt Bissonnette, a.k.a. Mark Owen, interview with Scott Pelley, *60 Minutes,* CBS, September 9, 2012.

138   **"I want you to think of two words":** Josh Nelson, "First Lady Tells UNI Crowd They Live in 'Special Place,'" *Waterloo-Cedar Falls Courier,* May 7, 2011.

139   **"It's not right to not let the gays":** Zirin, *Game Over,* p. 159.

139   **Obama boasts:** Barack Obama interview with Bill Simmons, *B.S. Report Podcast,* Grantland.com, March 1, 2012.

139   **"We're the Miami Heat":** Jodi Kantor, "The Competitor in Chief," *New York Times,* September 2, 2012.

139   **David Cameron joins Obama:** Nicholas Watt, "Barack Obama Pushes the Protocol Boundaries for David Cameron," *Guardian,* March 13, 2012.

140   **"But I can tell you this":** Sean Sullivan, "Thune: I Could Beat Obama at Basketball," *Washington Post*, August 29, 2012.

140   **As Obama readies for his first debate:** Jonathan Alter, *The Center Holds: Obama and His Enemies* (New York: Simon and Schuster, 2013), p. 321.

140   **"isn't as good as he thinks he is":** Reuters TV via HuffingtonPost.com, "David Stern, NBA Commissioner, Says Obama's 'Not That Good' at Basketball," October 27, 2012.

140   **includes former Chicago Bulls great Scottie Pippen:** Chuck Todd, *The Stranger: Barack Obama in the White House* (New York: Little, Brown, 2014), p. 359.

140   **Pat Kelsey broaches the school shootings:** "Pat Kelsey Makes Passionate Speech," ESPN.com, December 19, 2012.

141   **"It's your world":** Andrew Sharp, "Barack Obama to LeBron James: 'It's Your World, Man,'" SBNation.com, January 28, 2013.

141 **"wants Obama to do one thing"**: Kari Rea, "Dennis Rodman: Kim Jong-un Wants President Obama to 'Call Him,'" ABCNews.com, March 3, 2013.

141 **"I am wearing a green tie"**: Cindy Boren, "Obama Doesn't Like Notre Dame's Uniforms . . . So He's Getting One," *Washington Post*, March 21, 2013.

141 **"For his next pickup game"**: Tweet from @NDMikeBrey, March 20, 2013.

141 **the president telephones:** Sam Stein and Amanda Terkel, "Obama Calls Jason Collins, 'Impressed By His Courage' in Coming Out," HuffingtonPost.com, April 29, 2013.

141 **the First Lady sends out:** Tweet from @FLOTUS, April 29, 2013.

141 **"the most embarrassing moment"**: "ESPN's Kornheiser: Obama's Basketball Blunder 'Most Embarrassing Moment of His Presidency," RealClearPolitics.com, April 2, 2013.

141 **"best left-handed shameless gunner"**: David Martosko, "Host of San Francisco Fundraiser Uses Basketball Metaphor and Calls Obama 'the Best Left-Handed Shameless Gunner in the World'—after He Shot 2-for-22 at Monday's White House Exhibition," *Daily Mail*, December 31, 2013.

141 **"My shot's broke"**: Katie Zezima, "Obama Admits His Basketball Shot Is 'Broke,'" *Washington Post*, July 24, 2014.

141 **Obama becomes fascinated by:** Daniel Brown, "Obama Likes Stanford Grad's Hoops Revolution Theory," *San Jose Mercury News*, June 7, 2013.

142 **"A bunch of old guys"**: Ruth Tam, "Obama's Top Five Zingers on 'The Tonight Show,'" *Washington Post*, August 7, 2013.

142 **The administration advertises:** Natalie Villacorta, "Basketball Players Make Health Care Pitch," Politico.com, January 16, 2014.

142 **During a private meeting:** Pamela McClintock, "Obama: I Want to Host ESPN's 'SportsCenter' When I Retire," HollywoodReporter.com, December 4, 2013.

143 **"If a jayvee team"**: David Remnick, "Going the Distance: On and Off the Road with Barack Obama," *New Yorker*, January 27, 2014.

143 **former Purdue star Curt Clawson:** "Florida House Candidate Launches Full Court Press Super Bowl Ad in Hoops Challenge to Obama," FoxNews.com, February 3, 2014.

143 **A life-sized, custom-baked cookie:** Joe Coscarelli, "Belgium Atones for Racist Obama Caricatures with Racist Giant Cookie," *New York*, March 25, 2014.

144 **The league counts 25 percent:** Amanda Hess, "The WNBA Finally Recognizes Its Lesbian Fans," Slate.com, June 11, 2014.

144 **hasn't left the White House:** Jennifer Epstein, "Obama's New Teammate: Alonzo Mourning," Politico.com, June 1, 2014.

144   **"There is no doubt"**: Arden Farhi, "Why Obama Loves Golf, Basketball and All Things Athletic," CBSNews.com, December 26, 2014.

144   **"You know, he might"**: Catherine Thompson, "Obama Dishes It Right Back to Michael Jordan: Worry about Your NBA Team," TalkingPointsMemo.com, November 5, 2014.

145   **Krzyzewski implicitly criticizes:** Jordan Schachtel, "Duke's Coach K Delivers Scathing Critique of Obama Foreign Policy," Breitbart.com, November 5, 2014.

145   **less golf and more basketball:** Edward Alden, "Obama Needs to Forget Golf and Bring Back His Basketball Hustle," *Washington Post,* November 13, 2014.

145   **At a cabinet meeting:** Evan Osnos, "In the Land of the Possible," *New Yorker,* December 22 and 29, 2014.

145   **"Everybody wanted Michael Jordan":** Frank Rich, "In Conversation: Chris Rock," *New York,* November 30, 2014.

145   **"You know what?":** Amanda Hess, "Watch President Obama Break Down Stereotypes about Toys for Girls and Boys," Slate.com, December 24, 2014.

145   **"Credit to him":** Adam Silver, "Political Expression and Activism in Today's NBA," panel at Princeton University, MediaCentralLive.Princeton.edu, March 24, 2015.

146   **"We tried using State Troopers":** "Gov. Andrew Cuomo's Eulogy for His Father Mario Cuomo," Blogs.WSJ.com, January 6, 2015.

146   **After declining:** Jeremy Stahl, "Mitt Romney's Final NCAA Bracket Was Frighteningly Accurate," Slate.com, April 7, 2015.

147   **"Air POTUS":** Tweet from @WhiteHouse, May 8, 2015.

147   **Speaking with Marc Maron:** Barack Obama interview with Marc Maron, *WTF* podcast, June 22, 2015.

147   **"My best week, I will tell you":** Marina Koren and Matt Berman, "President Obama Reflects on His 'Best Week,'" NationalJournal.com, June 30, 2015.

147   **Harper publishes *You Don't Have to Live Like This*:** Benjamin Markovits, "An Impromptu (and Fictional) Game of Hoops with Barack Obama," Deadspin.com, May 1, 2015.

SELECTED BIBLIOGRAPHY

Alter, Jonathan. *The Center Holds: Obama and His Enemies*. New York: Simon and Schuster, 2013.

Axelrod, David. *Believer: My Forty Years in Politics*. New York: Penguin Press, 2015.

Boller, Paul F., Jr. *Presidential Diversions: Presidents at Play from George Washington to George W. Bush*. Orlando: Harcourt, 2007.

FreeDarko Presents. *The Undisputed Guide to Pro Basketball History*. New York: Bloomsbury, 2010.

Geithner, Timothy F. *Stress Test: Reflections on Financial Crises*. New York: Crown, 2014.

Glauberman, Stu, and Jerry Burns. *The Dream Begins: How Hawai'i Shaped Barack Obama*. Honolulu: Watermark, 2008.

Heilemann, John, and Mark Halperin. *Game Change: Obama and the Clintons, McCain and Palin, and the Race of a Lifetime*. New York: Harper, 2010.

Kantor, Jodi. *The Obamas*. New York: Back Bay Books, 2012.

Love, Reggie. *Power Forward: My Presidential Education*. New York: Simon and Schuster, 2015.

Mandelbaum, Michael. *The Meaning of Sports: Why Americans Watch Baseball, Football, and Basketball and What They See When They Do*. New York: PublicAffairs, 2005.

Maraniss, David. *Barack Obama: The Story*. New York: Simon and Schuster Paperbacks, 2012.

Mencken, H. L. *The Days of H. L. Mencken: Happy Days, Newspaper Days, Heathen Days*. New York: Alfred A. Knopf, 1947.

Mendell, David. *Obama: From Promise to Power*. New York: Amistad, 2007.

Obama, Barack. *The Audacity of Hope: Thoughts on Reclaiming the American Dream*. New York: Three Rivers Press, 2006.

————. *Dreams from My Father: A Story of Race and Inheritance*. New York: Three Rivers Press, 1995.

Owen, Mark. *No Easy Day: The Autobiography of a Navy Seal*. New York: Dutton, 2012.

Remnick, David. *The Bridge: The Life and Rise of Barack Obama*. New York: Knopf, 2010.

Robinson, Craig. *A Game of Character: A Family Journey from Chicago's Southside to the Ivy League and Beyond*. New York: Gotham, 2010.

Silber, William L. *Volcker: The Triumph of Persistence*. New York: Bloomsbury, 2012.

Slevin, Peter. *Michelle Obama: A Life*. New York: Knopf, 2015.

Taylor, Paul, and the Pew Research Center. *The Next America: Boomers, Millennials and the Looming Generational Showdown*. New York: PublicAffairs, 2014.

Todd, Chuck. *The Stranger: Barack Obama in the White House*. New York: Little, Brown, 2014.

Van Natta, Don, Jr. *First off the Tee: Presidential Hackers, Duffers and Cheaters from Taft to Bush*. New York: PublicAffairs, 2003.

Watterson, John Sayle. *The Games Presidents Play: Sports and the Presidency*. Baltimore: Johns Hopkins University Press, 2009.

Wolffe, Richard. *Renegade: The Making of a President*. New York: Crown, 2009.

Zirin, Dave. *Game Over: How Politics Has Turned the Sports World Upside Down*. New York: New Press, 2013.

INDEX

Page numbers in italics refer to photos.

Abdul-Jabbar, Kareem, 115, 133, 146
Affordable Care Act, 60–63, 135, 142, 143,
    147
Alagappan, Muthu, 141
Alan Parsons Project, 38, 131
Albert, Marv, 69
Albright, Madeleine, 94
Alden, Edward, 71, 109, 145
Allen, George, 2
Allen, Ray, 51, 52, 63, 108
Amaechi, John, 138
Anderson, Alan, 118
Anderson, Kenny, 93
Anthony, Carmelo, 51, 137
Archibald, Nate (Tiny), 133
Arenas, Gilbert, 51
Artest, Ron, 111
Asian Americans, 59, 67, *112,* 135
Atlanta Hawks, 2, 119–120
Attack Athletics (Chicago), 45, 72, 133
The Audacity of Hope (Obama), 15
Auerbach, Red, 112
Auriemma, Geno, 97

Axelrod, David, 6, 36, 38, 77, 136; and
    Obama debate with McCain, 45, 132; and
    presidential bracket, *74–75, 75,* 77

Baby Boomers, 10, 12, 52
Bae, Kenneth, 93, 94
Baker, Vin, 93
Baller-in-Chief website, 6, 69
Baracketology, *74,* 75–77, 133
The Barack Obama Basketball Mixtape, 28
Barber, Anthony (Cat), 76
Barea, J. J., 64
Barkley, Charles, 120
Bartolotta, Jimmy, 104
Barton, Joe, 121
Battier, Shane, 28, 63, 137
Belgian government gift of *speculaas* cookie,
    64, 143
Belinelli, Marco, 102
Berlusconi, Silvio, 64, *68,* 134
Biden, Joe, 59, 77, 97, 133
Biden, Maisy, 77
Billups, Chauncey, 51, 118, 137

Bing, Dave, 116, 135
bin Laden, Osama, 76, 116, 138
Bird, Larry, 111
Birthday celebrations, basketball games in,
    28, 52, *52–53,* 137, 142, 144
Birth of Barack Obama, 17
Bissonnette, Matt, 116, 138
Black Law Students Association, 23, 78, 130
Bloomberg BusinessWeek, 136, *136*
Boeheim, Jim, 116
Boehner, John, 89, 140
Bogues, Muggsy, 85
Boozer, Carlos, 52
Boston Celtics, *14,* 51, 77, 78, 112, 136, 142
Bourke, James, *3*
Bradley, Bill, 36, 89
Branch, Taylor, 120
Brand, Myles, 121
Brat, David, 105
Brazil, U.S. national team exhibition game
    against, *70, 110*
Brey, Mike, 141
Brooklyn Nets, 67, 113, 118, 134

Brown, Michael, 56, 118
Brown, Scott, 135
Brown University, Robinson at, 33
Bryant, Kobe, 63, 100, 111, 112, 137
Buckner, Quinn, 5
The Buried Life television show, 90, 135, *135*
Burke, Doris, 75
Burma, 67
Bush, George W., 2, 64, 76, 98, 108
Bush, Jeb, 76
Buss, Jeanie, 113
Butler University, 136
Bynum, Andrew, *8*
Bzomowski, Steve, 86, 87

Cameron, David, 47, 64, *69*, 139
Campaigning, role of basketball in, 2, 35–52, 130–131
Camp Arifjan (Kuwait), *41*, 44, 132
Camp David basketball games, *58–59*, 90–91, 144
Cantor, Eric, 105
Carlesimo, P. J., 111
Carlin, Robert, 94
Carrier Classic (2011), *54–55*
Carril, Pete, 12
Carson, Harry, 98
Carter, Jimmy, 2, 107
Carter, Vince, 30, *44*, 52, 118–119
Casey, Robert, 45, 77–78, *78*, 108
Catchings, Tamika, *38*
CBS, *13*, 122, *122*
Challenge for Change tournament, *38*, 41
Chalmers, Mario, 98
Chandler, Rod, 89
Chapman, Rex, 5
Charles, Tina, 97
Charleston church shootings, 56
Cheadle, Don, *11*, 12
Chicago, 2, 15, *24–25*, 25–27, 80; community organizing work in, 2, 15, 23; Election Day

basketball in, 45, 72, 78, 80, 133, 140; pickup games in, 2, 25–26, 78, 80
Chicago Bulls, 77, 86, 98, 136, 140; Jordan with, 38, 80; Noah with, 52, 112; Obama as fan of, *7*, 46, 52, 97; pregame music of, 38, 131; Rodman with, 93, 94; Rose with, 52, 117, *117*, 145
China, 67
Cho, Rich, 67, 113
Christie, Doug, 93
Clawson, Curt, 60, 105, 143
Clay, Ray, 38, 131
Cleveland Cavaliers, 51, 118, 133
Clinton, Bill, 2, 9, 41, 50, 63, 89
Clinton, Hillary, 35, 38, 64–65, 105, 131
Clooney, George, *11*, 12, 80–81
Coates, Ta-Nehisi, 55
College athletic programs, 120–122; graduation standards of, 87, 121, 135
Collier, Devon, 33
Collins, Jarron, 118
Collins, Jason, 60, 113, 114, *115*, 118, 141
Columbia University, Obama at, 23, 129
Congressional All-Star Classic (2010), *104*
Conlon, Marty, 67
Coolidge, Calvin, 98
Cornyn, John, 60
Cowherd, Colin, 63
Cuba, 147
Cunningham, Billy, 5
Cunningham, Jared, 33
Cuomo, Andrew, 146
Cuomo, Mario, 146

Dale, Norman (*Hoosiers* character), 41
Dallas Mavericks, 51, 64, *65*
Darrow, Mack, 85, 144
Davis, Al, 18
Davis, Baron, 51
Dayton (Ohio) NCAA tournament game, 64, *69*, 139

De Carolis, Bob, 33
Decerega, Rey, 90–92, 137
Delany, Veronica, *3*
Democratic National Conventions, 31, 33, *42*, 46, 130
Deng, Luol, 119
Dent, Charlie, 121
Denver Nuggets, *42*, 51, 113
DePauw University Tigers White House visit, *98*, 99
Detroit Pistons, 51, 93, 98, 111, 117, 118, 135
DeVaughn, William, 19
Diaw, Boris, 102
Dieng, Gorgui, 64
Diggins, Skylar, 85, 143
Donovan, Sean, 134
Dooling, Keyon, 138
Dowd, Matthew, 112
Downey, Tom, 89
Drake Group, 120, 121
Dreams from My Father (Obama), 6, 9, 18
Duhon, Chris, 6
Duke University, *13*, 46, 63, 119, 136; Krzyzewski as coach at, 46, 59, 136, 145; Love as basketball player at, 5, 36, 46, 47, 77, 130; White House visit from NCAA championship team, *99*
Duncan, Arne, 85–87, 90, 130; criticisms of NCAA, 87, 121, 122, 135; in Fort McNair game, 91; in Haiti, *84*; at Harvard, 12, 136, 139; in NBA All-Star Weekend Celebrity Game, 85, 143; on playing style of Obama, 26; as regular in presidential pickup games, *4–5*, 31, *87*, 134; as Secretary of Education, 12, 26, 77, 85, 86–87, 136; in three-on-three tournaments, 12, 82, 85, 144
Duncan, Sue, 26, 86
Duncan, Tim, 6, 97, *113*
Dunham, Ann, 17
Dunham, Stan, 128

Earnest, Josh, 100, 102
Eisenhower, Dwight, 2, 108–109
"Elbowgate," 92
Election Day basketball games, 45, 72, 78, 80, 131, 132, 133, 140
Empowering Girls and Women through Sports initiative, 67
Erving, Julius, 6, 19, 49
ESPN, 2, 33, 72, 75, 76, 77; *SportsCenter* program, 60, 72, 135, 142
Everett, Van, *iv*
Ewing, Patrick, 52

Feaster, Allison, 67
Feldstein, Andrew, 25
Fernandez, John, 46
Ferry, Danny, 119–120
Flake, Jeff, 104, *104*
Floyd, Sleepy, 93
Foley, James, 108
Ford, Gerald, 2, 12, 121
Foreign policy, 63–69; Cuba in, 147; North Korea in, 93–94, *95*, 141
Fort McNair basketball games: on birthday, *52–53*, 137; mouth injury during, 71, 90–92, *91*, 108, 137
Frakes, Bill, 49
Francis, Steve, 51
Freeman, Jerome (Hook), 18
Frese, Brenda, 76
Friedlander, Justin, 137

Game of Change, *101*, 142
Gantt, Harvey, 116, 130
Garner, Eric, 56, 117, *117*, 145
Garnett, Kevin, 51, 118
Gasol, Pau, *8*, 137
Gay athletes, 113, 114, *115*, 138, 141, 144
G-8 summit meeting in Italy, 64, *68*, 134
Geithner, Pete, 78
Geithner, Timothy, 78, 134

Genachowski, Julius, 25, 44, 78, 132
Generation Jones, 10
Georgetown University, *13*
Giannoulias, Alexi, 45, *78*, 78, 131, 140
Gibbs, Robert, *74–75*, 75
Gillard, Julia, 64
Gingrich, Newt, 105
Ginobili, Manu, 97, 102, *113*
Gleason, Jackie, 12
Global Sports Mentoring Program, 67
Gold, Joe Dan, 142
Golden State Warriors, 111, 133
Golf, 69, 71, *106–107*, 107–109, 145; playing partners in, *62*, 71, 80, 108, 144
Goodell, Roger, 60
Gordon, Derrick, 114, 144
Gore, Al, 89
Grayson, Trey, 136
Griner, Brittney, 144
Grunfeld, Ernie, 29
Gus Macker three-on-three tournaments, 9

Hackman, Gene, 41
Haiti, *85*
Ham, Darvin, 67
Hammon, Becky, 102, 113
Hansbrough, Tyler, *34–35*, 41, 131
Hardaway, Penny, 52
Hardaway, Tim, 138–139
Harkness, Jerry, *101*, 142
Harper, Hill, 23, 78–79, 130
Harper, Stephen, 64
Harvard Law Review, 23, 25, 78
Harvard Law School, 15, 23, 25, 78, 130
Hawaii: early life of Obama in, 17–23; golfing in, *106–107*; Punahou School in (*see* Punahou School [Honolulu, Hawaii])
Hawkins, Connie, 133
Health insurance reform, 60–63, 135, 142, 143
Heaven Is a Playground (Telander), 128
Heilemann, John, 105

Helms, Jesse, 116
Hemenway Gym at Harvard Law School, 23, 25, 78
High school basketball at Punahou School, 6, 9, 12, 17, 18–23, 129, 147
Hill, Baron, 89
Hill, Grant, 60, *62*, 119, 137
Hodges, Craig, 93
Holder, Eric, 79, 90, 133
Holiday, Dwight, 18
Hoop-It-Up three-on-three tournaments, 9, 85
Hoops for Hope Congressional All-Star Classic (2010), *104*
Hoosiers (film), 41, 136
Hoover, Herbert, 2
Hope, Bob, 12
Hopper, Dennis, 41
H-O-R-S-E games, 41, *47, 57,* 69, 124, 134
Houston Rockets, 51
Howard, Juwan, 46

"I Can't Breathe" shirt, 117, *117,* 145
Iger, Bob, 142
Ilunga-Mbenga, Didier, *8*
Immigration legislation, 113, 114, *114,* 136
Indiana, *36–37, 38–39,* 41, 45, 132, 133, 146
Indiana Basketball Hall of Fame, *38–39,* 41
Inslee, Jay, 133
Interior Department basketball court, *71,* 81, 82, *87,* 89
International relations, 63–69; Cuba in, 147; North Korea in, 93–94, *95,* 141
Iowa, 38, 45, 131; driveway game with McIntosh family in, *56*; one-on-one game with Price in, *48–49, 49–50,* 131
Irving, Kyrie, 118
ISIS, 59, 108, 143, 145
Istanbul, Archbishop of, 64, 134
Italy, basketball at G-8 summit meeting in, 64, *68,* 134
Iverson, Allen, 30, 105, 112, 133

Jack, Jarrett, 118
Jackson, Arthur, 31, 69, 89, 90, 91, 92, 108
Jackson, Phil, 100, *100*
James, LeBron, 64, 137; on Cleveland Cav-
    aliers, 51, 118, 133; on Miami Heat, 98,
    117, 141; political activism of, 51, 60, 63,
    117, 118; on U.S. national team, *110*; White
    House visit after NBA championship, 98,
    141
Johnson, Claude, 6, 9, 69, 71
Johnson, Kevin, 116, 133
Johnson, Magic, 29, 52, 62, 63, 111, 114–115,
    116, 143
Jones, James, 79
Jordan, Michael, 111, 144; as apolitical, 116,
    130; with Chicago Bulls, 38, 80; and Dun-
    can, 85; and North Korea, 94; as Obama
    supporter, 52, 118–119, 130; and Rogers, 82

Kamana, John, 20
Katz, Andy, *74–75*, 75–76, 133
Keibler, Stacy, *11*
Kellogg, Clark, *13*
Kelsey, Pat, 116, 140
Kennedy, Edward, 135
Kennedy, John F., 5, 50
Kerry, John, 80
Key, Keegan-Michael, 56
Khosla, Neal, 141
Khosla, Vinod, 141
Kikwete, Jakaya, 64
Kim Jong-chul, 94
Kim Jong-un, 93–94, *95*, 141
King, John, 6
King, Stacey, 80
Kirkpatrick, Kip, 80
Kiss Cam, *70*, 120
Klain, Ron, 140
Klosterman, Chuck, 33
Koch brothers, 104, *105*
Kohl, Herb, 79, 133
Kornheiser, Tony, 141

Krzyzewski, Mike, 46, 59, 136, 145
Kuwait, Obama sinking three-pointer in, 6,
    41, 44, 105, 132

LaHood, Ray, 90
Laimbeer, Bill, 98
Landau, Susan, 77
Leblanc, Rita Benson, 113
Lee, Spike, 30, *44*
Left-handedness, 28, 29, *71*, 97, 140, 141
Leno, Jay, 75
Lenox, Max, 145
Let's Move anti-obesity initiative, 60
Levenson, Bruce, 119–120
Lewis, Michael, 27, 90
Limbaugh, Rush, 76
Lin, Jeremy, 59, *112*, 113, 139
Lincoln, Abraham, 41
Lobo, Rebecca, 75
Los Angeles, pickup game in, *11*
Los Angeles Clippers, 113, 117, 119, 124
Los Angeles Lakers, *8*, 59, 67, 100, *100*, 111,
    113, 115, 137
Los Suns uniforms, 113, *114*, 136
Love, Reggie, 46–47, *47*, 69, 90, *112*, 121,
    135; as Duke basketball player, 5, 36, 46,
    47, 77, 130; at Fort McNair game, 91, 92;
    on international influence of basketball,
    64; Krzyzewski as coach of, 46, 59; in New
    Hampshire game, 36, 130; and presiden-
    tial bracket in NCAA tournament, *74–75*;
    as regular in presidential pickup games,
    viii, *4–5*, *14*, 31, 47, *87*, *88*, 108, 124, 134;
    talking trash with Obama, 30; as youth
    coach, 71, *72–73*, 138
Loyola 1963 NCAA championship team, 99,
    101, 142
Lundquist, Verne, *13*

Magic Johnson Enterprises, 115
Maguire, Tobey, *11*, 12
Mahorn, Rick, 98

Mandelbaum, Michael, 12
Maraniss, David, 12
Markey, Ed, 89
Markovits, Benjamin, 147
Maron, Marc, 147
Marshall, Josh, 118
Martin, Trayvon, 56, 113–114, 117, 139
Max, Tucker, 26, 29
May, Shayna Barry, *43*
McCain, Cindy, 75
McCain, John, 30, 41, *44*, 45, 105, 132
McCarthy, Kevin, 75
McConnell, Mitch, 60, 80
McDaniel, Chris, 105–106
McGee, JaVale, 7
McIntosh family (Harrison County, Iowa), *56*
McLachlin, Chris, 6, 9, 18, 19, 20–22, *21*
Mencken, H. L., 107
Merkel, Angela, 64, *65*
Miami Heat, 59, 60, 63, 98, 113, 139; James
    with, 98, 117, 141; White House visits by,
    98, 141
Michigan State in Carrier Classic, *54–55*
Millennials, 52, 56, 63, 116–117
Mills, Patty, 64, 102, 139
Milwaukee Bucks, 79, 114, 133, 138
Misaka, Wat, 135
Monroe, Greg, 117
Montgomery, Renee, 97
Moore, Craig, 85, 144
Moore, Maya, 97, 137
Moran, Jim, 121
Mourning, Alonzo, 52, 60, 62, *62*, 137, 143; as
    golfing partner, *62*, 71, 108, 144
Mouth injury at Fort McNair game, 71, 90–
    92, *91*, 108, 137
Mutombo, Dikembe, *14*, 51, 147
My Brother's Keeper initiative, 56, 124
Myers, DeeDee, 89

Nantz, Jim, 122
Napier, Shabazz, 121, 122, *122*

Napolitano, Janet, 79, 79
Nash, Bob, 18
Nash, Steve, 6, *114*, 136, 147
NBA, 2, *8*, 59, 111–120; activism of players in, 113–119; All-Star Weekend (2009), 6; All-Star Weekend (2014) Celebrity Game, 85, 143; Asian Americans in, 59, 67, *112*; international influence of, 64, 65, *65*, 66, 67; management of, 119–120; and North Korea, 93–94; and Obamacare promotions, 60, 62, 63; player support for Obama, 51–52, 62, *62*, 112; and SportsUnited programs, 65; White House visits from champions of, 99, 141. *See also specific teams*
NCAA, 120–122; graduation standards of, 87, 121, 135
NCAA basketball tournament, 18, 64; Cameron and Obama attending, 64, *69*; Obama picks in, 2, 62–63, 64, *74*, 75–77, 133, 134; Romney picks in, 76, 146–147; White House visits from winners of, 97–98, 99, *101*, 142
Nelson, Roberto, 33
Nesbitt, Alex, 80
Nesbitt, Marty, 26, 45, 72, 79–80, *80*, 87, 137
Nevada election results, 45, 131
Newhall, Eric, 23
New Hampshire, 35–36, 38, 45, 46, 130, 131
Newtown (Connecticut) school shootings, 116, 140
New York Knicks, *44*, 59, *112*, 135, 139
Nicholson, Marvin, 80
Nike shoes, 94, 133, 147
Nixon, Richard, 2, 50
Noah, Joakim, 52, *52–53*, 112
Nocera, Joe, 120
Noland, Ray, *43*
North Carolina, *34–35*, 41, 45, 46, 133
North Carolina Tar Heels. *See* University of North Carolina Tar Heels
North Korea, 93–94, *95*, 141
Notre Dame, 134, 141
Nowitzki, Dirk, 51, 64, *65*

Oakley, Charles, 5
Obama, Barack, Sr., *16*, 17; basketball gift from, 18, 128
Obama, Malia, *14, 71*, 147
Obama, Michelle, 2, 25–26, 30, 31, 49, 63, 130, 138, 147; at Carrier Classic, *54–55*; Let's Move anti-obesity initiative of, 60; at Verizon Center, *110*
Obama, Sasha, *14, 71*, 147; basketball team of, 71, 72, *72–73*, 77, 138
Obamacare, 60–63, 135, 142, 143
Obama Classic, 119
ObamaGolfCounter website, 108
"Obama Got Next" poster, *43*
Occidental College, 23, 129
Okur, Mehmet, 64
O'Neal, Shaquille, 51, 64
O'Neill, Tip, 89
One-on-one games with Price, *48–49*, 49–50, 131
Oregon State University, Robinson at, 31–33, *32*, 75, 99
Orlando Magic, 51
Orme, Greg, 80
Owen, Mark, 116, 138
Oxley, Mike, 89

Palin, Sarah, 9, 104, 132
Panetta, Leon, 137
Parker, Tony, 46, 97, 102, *113*
Paul, Chris, 46, 52, 60, 119, 124, *125*, 137
Paul, James, 52
Paul, Rand, 76, 136
Pavlova, Irina, 113
Penebacker, John, 18
Penicheiro, Ticha, 147
Peterson, Tony, 128
Pfeiffer, Dan, 80, *80*
Phoenix Suns, 6, 113, 114, *114*, 136
Pickup games, 9–12, 19, 69, 89–90, 134; in campaigning, 45, 77; in Chicago, 2, 25–26, 78, 80; Duncan and Love as regulars in,

viii, 4–5, 14, 31, 47, *87, 88*, 108, 124, 134; at Harvard, 44, 78; in Los Angeles, *11*; mouth injury in, 71, 90–92, *91*, 108, 137; at Occidental College, 129; playing style in, 5, 30–31, 108; rib injury in, 78, 131; in Walpole prison, 23, 78, 130
Pierce, Paul, 52
Pippen, Scottie, 72, 140
Playing style, *28*, 28–31, *29, 30*, 50; left-handed, 28, 29, *71*, 97, 140, 141; and race, 5–6
Podlogar, Alex, 41, 109
Pontell, Jonathan, 10
Popovich, Gregg, 97
Portman, Rob, 76
Powell, Colin, 75
Power, Samantha, *3*, 80–81
Presidency of Obama, 55–109; coaching of youth team during, 71–72, *72–73*; health care reform during, 60–63, 135, 142, 143; international relations during, 63–69, 93–94, *95*, 141, 147; Love as assistant in, 46–47, 69; NBA during, 111–120; NCAA during, 120–122; NCAA tournament picks during, *74*, 75–77; opponents with basketball connections, 104–106; supporters with basketball connections, 77–90; therapeutic role of basketball during, 69; transition to golf during, 69, 71, *106–107*, 107–109, 144, 145; White House visits of championship teams during, *96*, 97–102, *98, 99, 101, 103*
Presidential Medal of Freedom, 99, 142
President's Council on Fitness, Sports and Nutrition, 60, *62*
Price, Jack, 49
Price, S. L. (Scott), *48–49*, 49–50, 131
Princeton University, 31, 33, 76, 81; Craig Robinson at, 12, 25, 26, 31, 81, 85, 130; Leslie Robinson at, 100, 146; Rogers at, 12, 26, 31, 81, 85, 130; Stengel at, 142; Volcker at, 82
Pritzker, Penny, 26

Prokhorov, Mikhail, 134
Punahou School (Honolulu, Hawaii), 128; Obama on basketball team of, 6, 9, 12, 17, 18–23, *21*, 129, 147; Obama speech at (2004), 20; Orme and Ramos as students at, 80
Putin, Vladimir, 134

Racial issues, 55–59, 105–106; and identity of Obama, 19, 22; in NBA, 112, 119–120; and playing style, 5–6, 19
Ramos, Mike, 80
Rawls, Miles, 7
Reagan, Ronald, 98, 123
Reed, Ishmael, 6
Reinsdorf, Jerry, 136
Remnick, David, 59
Republican Party, 104–106, 140
Rib injury in pickup game, 78, 131
Rice, John, 81, 91
Rice, Susan, 81, *81*, 90, 91
Ri Myong Hun (Michael Ri), 94
The Rise of Barack Obama (Souza), 123
Roberts, Michele, 113
Roberts, Pat, 89
Robinson, Cliff, 93
Robinson, Craig, 1, 10, 19, 31–33, 44, 79; evaluating Obama as potential brother-in-law, 2, 25–26, 31, 82, 130; as NBA draft pick, 77; at Oregon State, 31–33, *32*, 75, 99; on playing style of Obama, 28, 29, 30, 31; at Princeton, 12, 25, 26, 31, 81, 85, 130
Robinson, Fraser, 25, 31
Robinson, Leslie, 100, 146
Robinson, Marian, *33–34*
Robinson, Michelle, 25–26. *See also* Obama, Michelle
Rock, Chris, 145
Rodgers, Cathy McMorris, 76
Rodman, Dennis, 93–94, *95*, 141
Rodriguez, Matt, 35, 36, 38, 130
Rogers, John, 12, 26, 31, 81–82, *82*, 85, 86, 130

Romney, Mitt, 59, 62, 76, 139, 140; NCAA tournament picks of, 76, 146–147
Rooney family, 100
Roosevelt, Teddy, 2, 59
Rose, Derrick, 52, *52–53*, 117, 137; wearing "I Can't Breathe" shirt, 117, *117*, 145
Rotella, Carlo, 85
Rouse, Pete, 46
Rove, Karl, 105
Rubio, Marco, 76
Rush, Bobby, 121
Russell, Bill, *14*, 52, 99, 142
Ryan, Evan, 65–67
Ryan, Paul, 76

Salazar, Ken, 82, 134
Same-sex marriage, 147
San Antonio Spurs, *96*, 97, 100, 102, 113, *113*, 146
Sarver, Robert, 114, 136
Scalise, Steve, 60
Schmiel, Eugene, 93
Schumer, Charles, 83
Schwarzenegger, Arnold, 105, 132
Scott, Bobby, 121
Seal Team Six, 116, 138
Seattle SuperSonics, 30
Senate term of Obama, 46
Shimkus, John, 106
Shuler, Heath, 89
Sidley Austin law firm, 25
Silas, Paul, 5
Silver, Adam, 113, 117–118, 119, *119*, 120, 145
Silver, Nate, 75
Singer, Jonathan, *42*
Slam magazine, 6, 28
Smith, Ariyana, 118
Smith, Charles, 93
Smith, Dean, 41, 142
Smith, Kenny, 120
Smith, Linnea, 142

Sneakers: custom, *43*; Nike, 94, 133, 147
Soetoro, Lolo, 17
Soetoro-Ng, Maya, 12, 33
Souza, Pete, 69, 71, 92, *123*, 123–124
Spencer, Iowa, one-on-one game with Price in, *48–49*, 49–50, 131
Splitter, Tiago, 102
Spoelstra, Erik, 63
SportsCenter program, 60, 72, 135, 142
Sports Envoys program, 65, 67
SportsUnited programs, 65–67
Sports Visitors program, 65, 67
Sprewell, Latrell, 111
Staley, Dawn, 52
Starn, Orin, 45
State of the Union (2015) address, 60
Stengel, Richard, 142
Sterling, Donald, 117, 119
Stern, David, 60, 112, 115, 119, 120, 140
Stevens, Brad, 136
Steyer, Tom, 141
Strautmanis, Michael, 137
Summitt, Pat, 99, 139
Sunstein, Cass, *3*
Super Tuesday, 38, 45
Supreme Court, 147; and "highest court in the land," 78, 89
Swoopes, Sheryl, 52, 144
Sykes, Wanda, 134

Taft, William Howard, 107
Tavares, Larry, 129
Team Ariel, 82, 85
"Team Captain" doll, *43*
Telander, Rick, 29, 128
Television, Obama watching, 72
Thibodeau, Tom, 86, 136
Thomas, Etan, 60, 137
Three-on-three tournaments, 9–10; Challenge for Change, *38*, 41; Duncan in, 82, 85, 144; Hoop-It-Up, 9, 85; Team Ariel in, 82, 85

Thune, John, 104, *104*, 140
Today television show, 45
The Tonight Show, 75, 142
Trammell, Jack, 105
Trans-Pacific trade authority, 147
Trash-talking, 30
Truman, Harry, 2, 107
Turkoglu, Hedo, 64

Ujiri, Masai, 113
University of Chicago Law School, 26–27, 29, 78
University of Connecticut: APR deficiency in, 121, *122*, 135; men's team as NCAA tournament champions, 121, *122*; women's basketball team, 97
University of Hawaii, 17, 18, 128
University of North Carolina Tar Heels, *34–35*, 41; in Carrier Classic, *54–55*; in NCAA tournament brackets, 64, 77, 98, 133, 134; Obama playing in scrimmage with, *34–35*, 41, 131; Smith as former coach of, 41, 142; White House visit by, 97–98, *102–103*
U.S. national basketball team, in exhibition game against Brazil, *70, 110*

Vaccaro, Sonny, 120
Verizon Center: Kiss Cam in, *70*; national team exhibition game in, *70, 110*
Villicana, Aaron, *36–37*
Vipers basketball team, 71, 72, 138
Virginia campaign rally, *40–41*
Volcker, Paul, 82, *82*

Wade, Dwyane, 60, 63, 98, 137
Walpole, Massachusetts, basketball game at prison in, 23, 78, 130
Wamp, Zach, 104
Wang Qishan, *66–67, 67*
Warner, Mark, 89
Washington Wizards, 7, 51, 60, 85
Webb, Spud, 55
The Week, 140
Weis, Frédéric, 30, *44*
Westhead, Paul, 140
The West Wing television show, 46
Whitaker, Eric, 23, 45, 82–83, *83*
White, Mary Jo, 83
White House: championship basketball teams visiting, *96*, 97–102, *98, 99, 101, 103*, 141, 142; Everett at, *iv*; Friedlander at, 137; Love at, *viii–ix*, 46–47, *47*; mentoring pro-

gram participants at, *57*; NBA players at, *8, 60, 62, 63*, 141; Power and Sunstein at, *3*; South Lawn tennis/basketball court, *viii–ix, xii, 57*, 69, *88*, 97, 134; Wang Qishan at, *66, 67*; Wounded Warriors game at, *60–61*
Wilkens, Lenny, 29, 30
Williams, Deron, *110*, 118
Williams, Jason, 5
Wilson, Ben, 85
WNBA, *38, 66, 67*, 98, 99, 102, 115, 144
Woodstock Generation, 10, 12
Wounded Warriors, *60–61*, 137
WTF podcast, 147

Xi Jinping, 67

You Don't Have to Live Like This (Markovits), 147
Young, Jitim, 85, 144
YouTube, *The Barack Obama Basketball Mixtape* on, 28

Zapatero, José Luis Rodríguez, 64
Zinn, Mike, 129
Zirin, Dave, 56
Zucker, Gillian, 113

New York Times best-selling author **Alexander Wolff** is a senior writer at *Sports Illustrated*, co-author (with Armen Keteyian) of *Raw Recruits*, and the author of *Big Game, Small World: A Basketball Adventure*. Visit him online at TheAudacityofHoop.com.